Nobody ever told her it would be like this!

When Debby Wood and her family moved to Florida four years ago, she envisioned daily baths in the fountain of youth, defying time and Mother Nature.

She figured a lovely tan, sun-bleached hair and a girlish figure just naturally went with the territory.

Now her hair is graying, her torso is spreading, and her tan is fading. The only baths she ever sees are in tubs with dirty rings and rubber duckies.

You're sure to see a little of yourself as you read how Debby stumbles into middle age and motherhood in this madcap collection of her stories.

Middle age & other spreads

by Debby Wood

Copyright© 1981 by Debby Wood
Cover art copyright© 1981 by Carmine Voli

All rights reserved. Reproduction or use in any manner without express permission is prohibited.

Library of Congress Catalog Number 81-70366

International Standard Book Number 0-9607490-0-4

A number of the chapters in this book are based on material that has appeared in the Lee County Shopper and in Home & Condo magazine.

Printed and bound in Florida, U.S.A.
The Graphic Press, Inc., Hollywood, Florida

To my husband,

who hit middle age two years before I did, but **he** doesn't have any gray hair to show for it!

Table of Contents

1. Nobody ever told me it'd be like this! — 11
2. Lost between little white gloves and see-through blouses — 15
3. You're worth your weight in gold — 18
4. The trick is knowing when to get away — 22
5. Who wrote 'wash me' on the bathroom mirror? — 25
6. Tempers flare on our barbecue grill! — 29
7. To love, honor, and take out the garbage — 32
8. Surviving germ warfare — 35
9. That must be someone else on my driver's license — 39
10. My balance of payments is a credit to MasterCard — 43
11. Some day my prints will come! — 46
12. Kids think a car is a wastebasket with wheels — 48
13. Who ever called summer a vacation? — 51
14. Over-sleeping can be alarming — 54
15. The way we were — 57
16. Don't all shirts come with ring around the collar? — 60
17. Watching the best years of our lives — 64
18. The vicious red fingernail set — 68
19. Table-top psychology: a lesson in good taste — 72
20. There's nothing wrong with being stacked — 75
21. I should have seen it coming when the moving van arrived! — 79
22. Bathroom battles make me flushed — 81
23. My house was designed by Frank Lloyd Wrong — 87

24. Florida's state pest is driving me buggy	90
25. Swap the Gulf for Lake Erie — you've got to be kidding!	93
26. You think you've got problems!	96
27. In hock, and stranded at the dock	101
28. Fishing in troubled waters	104
29. Cupid takes a holiday after the honeymoon.	108
30. Requiem for a guinea pig	111
31. Puppy love	115
32. Ho, ho, ho? No, no, no!	118
33. 'Tis the week after Christmas . . .	123

Introduction

Middle age is tough to define.

If you're 29, middle age is three years away and there's no need to worry.

If you're 34, middle age is still three years away, but it's time to start worrying.

If you're 39, you may think middle age is still three years away, but everyone around you knows the awful truth.

I never worried much about my age until I got my new driver's license this year. I was shocked.

"Whose picture is that on my license?" I shouted at the clerk. Her smile was devastating. Right then and there it hit me — I'd found middle age!

Actually, middle age is a state of mind.

My mother is still waiting for me to grow up, and my daughters think of me as an old lady. I guess that's what middle age is — somewhere in between, searching for a niche.

1
Nobody ever told me it'd be like this!

Only now, 14 years after graduating from college, do I realize that I was cheated on my education.

Instead of learning about Socrates and Margaret Mead, I should have been learning how to get bubble gum out of shag carpet.

What did Shakespeare ever teach me about felt-tip pen marks on blue velvet sofas? Shakespeare probably never even used a felt-tip pen.

While I was sleeping through Philosophy 101, I should have been studying up on how to find the mates for 16 black socks, and the most efficient way to fold three dozen pair of underwear.

And those hours spent in literature classes just didn't prepare me for the kinds of books I'm reading today: Babar's Birthday Surprise; The Velveteen Rabbit; Holly Hobbie's Nursery Rhymes. My sophomore English teacher didn't even mention Dr. Seuss when we were studying great authors.

I became fully aware of the problem the other day when I was trying to look up the spelling of a word. The only dictionary I could find in the house was "The First Golden Book Encyclopedia." Each word had a picture beside it.

I only took one economics class at college, but I do remember reading about guns and butter in the economic scheme of things. Somehow I never dreamed that the guns would be water pistols and the butter would be margarine.

Not once in that economics course did we broach the subject of shopping in the supermarket, and I consider that to be the biggest economic challenge today.

Of course, when I was in college, interest rates were hovering at 4 percent and Master Charge hadn't been invented yet. My kids find that hard to believe. I find it a little hard to believe myself!

Psychology might have been more useful if the teacher would have concentrated on child psychology rather than behavioral problems in rats. True, children and rats do sometimes exhibit the same behavioral problems, but at least you can learn to deal with rats.

I spent a good 50 to 60 hours in the psychology lab during my junior year studying mazes, testing, behavior and the senses. How was I to know then that life is simply a maze of dirty clothes, dirty dishes, and dirty children. The real test is maintaining your sense of humor!

I always had trouble with math in college, but not once did the professor deal with such important topics as balancing your checkbook. What good is algebra when it comes to trying to remember how much the check to the garden center was for?

What they should teach is a course in checkbook math that would cover everything from keeping check stubs to dreaming up excuses for overdrawn accounts. That course could probably save more marriages than all the marriage counseling outfits in the country.

After four years of French the only thing I remember how to say is "croissants," and that just gets me in trouble! Rather than studying a foreign

Nobody ever told me it'd be like this!

language, I should have studied baby-talk. Learning how to communicate with my children would have made the past few years a lot easier. I mean, just who cares what the French words for "moo cow" or "beddie-bye" are anyway?

I struggled through one semester of a speech course at college, but I still have trouble at the drive-in window of McDonald's. "I want one burger and two fries; no, make that two burgers and one fry; no, change that to a fish sandwich; wait, let's make it one burger and . . ."

My biology teacher forgot to teach me how to keep bugs out of the house, or how to keep my plants from drying up and falling out of the pots, or how to scrape mold off the bread without letting the kids see it first. Not once in biology did we discuss what to do when the water in the swimming pool turns brown!

And my chemistry professor never even mentioned the problems of mixing baby formula at 4 in the morning with one eye propped halfway open and one finger blistered from testing the scalding water.

Speaking of formulas, I should have been learning the formula for putting together a decent meal from three days of leftovers. Or why too much fertilizer kills plants. Or what to do when your child swallows a big swig of Formula 409.

The only chemistry I truly appreciate today is when the little blue crystals go into the toilet bowl, cause an explosion of bubbles, and disappear, leaving a clean toilet. That's what I call good chemistry!

Sociology could have covered a lot more than it did. For instance, how do other couples deal with the problem of sleeping in a bed where the blanket always disappears? Surely other civilizations have had to solve the problem of hogging the blanket. Has anyone ever come up with a solution? Sociology should have touched on other things, like the fight over who takes out the garbage every night, or how to survive a family vacation in the mountains, or should you take away the pacifier when your child reaches six. I personally would like to know more about those wonderful societies that send children away at the age of 12 and don't let them back home until they're adults and on their own.

The one college course I still get some benefit from is communications. Back then we called it journalism. And no, contrary to what my children will tell you, it was **NOT** before television was invented!

The problem is, my journalism teacher didn't tell us about the long hours and the low pay. He just told us about the glory and the excitement. Well, as I look around the dirty bedrom I use as an office, and see the stacks of clothes that need to be folded just outside the door, I realize that the glory and the excitement have worn a little thin.

Yes, when it comes to education, I was cheated.

I suspect that if I had spent four years studying home economics, I might have been a little better prepared for what was to come.

But if I knew then what I know now, I might just have decided to choose a different line of work — like home-building instead of home-making.

2
Lost between little white gloves and see-through blouses

There's something strange happening throughout the country today.

Everyday dozens of mothers go out to buy another box of diapers or another gallon of milk, and they never come back.

Somewhere between the store and the home, something snaps. Mother realizes there must be more to life than cleaning up spilled milk or making sure the family isn't afflicted with ring-around-the-collar. And so she ditches the diapers and heads off for a new life of fun and fulfillment.

To be honest, I can't say the thought has never crossed my mind. After all, when you're entering middle age and the only thing you have to show for it is a clean toilet bowl, reality can be devastating.

But equally devastating are all the stories I see about the "new mother," who is fun to be with and happy with herself. I read about the "Super Mom" and feel caught in a generation gap, lost somewhere between little white gloves and see-through blouses.

My biggest challenge this past year has been to pick up every piece of "grass" from Easter baskets and get it out of the house forever. You know how that stuff hides under sofas and behind the refrigerator. I never have been able to figure out why they can't invent a vacuum cleaner that can pick it up.

But during a recent visit to the doctor's office, I found myself reading an article in a woman's magazine explaining how to improve your sex life with the other kind of "grass."

Somewhere in between is where I want to be. But how do you get there?

Women's magazines are no help. They just make me feel inferior.

Who really wants to know about Buffy, who holds down a full-time job as a municipal court judge but still has time to whip up a gourmet meal for her family every night?

Buffy sends her children to school with lunch boxes filled with carrot sticks and crab meat and homemade chicken soup.

Buffy's husband wears freshly ironed shirts and his socks never have holes in the toes.

Buffy has a sensible wardrobe that she threw together herself on her little Singer sewing machine. She doesn't have bad breath in the morning, and she doesn't wear curlers at night.

And of course Buffy got a zero when she took the Ladies Home Journal test on sexual hangups. She has always had a fulfilling relationship with her husband.

Who needs Buffy? I certainly don't want to read about her. Frankly, I don't think Buffy has ever existed except in the mind of some demented magazine editor in New York City who is searching for a good psychiatrist.

When my friend Hortense got a job, she felt so bad about microwave dinners every night that she would stop at the store on the way home and load up on Sarah Lee desserts, just to ease her guilt a little bit. The kids loved it. They never had it so good!

Whenever I read about "Super Mom," I feel a generation behind the times.

Of course I realize we're not just talking about a generation gap, but a whole new attitude on the part of women. Just a few decades ago mothers were expected to stay at home and take care of the children and the housework.

But in the past few years, things have changed. For many families, it is an economic necessity for the wife to hold down a full-time job.

That has altered things at home and at the office. But more significantly, it has created confusion and conflict in the minds of many women.

I've decided that overcoming these conflicts is like learning to make hollandaise sauce. It takes plenty of time and practice. And it's bound to curdle now and then. But it is possible, no matter what stage of life you're in.

3
You're worth your weight in gold

At last, the truth is out.

According to Family Circle magazine, the value of the average full-time homemaker's work is $793.79 a week. That adds up to — count 'em fellas — more than $41,000 a year!

I always knew I was underpaid and overworked, but I never realized the severity of the problem.

It seems the average homemaker performs at least 22 separate functions around the home, with

You're worth your weight in gold

child care topping the list as the most time-consuming. The average homemaker spends 186 hours a week taking care of children. At a token $1 an hour, that adds up to over $9,000 each year. And that's not all. Seven hours a week cleaning the house at a minimum of $3.21 an hour is worth $22 a week. Cooking for 13 hours at a rate of $4.75 an hour is another $62 a week, and the three hours a week that a wife spends acting as a maid or hostess for her husband, at $20 an hour, adds another $60 to her wages.

The article certainly opened my eyes. Suddenly, I was worth my weight in gold. I began to think of myself as one of those high-priced executives.

Twenty hours a week driving the kids around is worth $100 in chauffeur's wages. Practical nurses get paid a fortune to administer health care as I do for my family. A psychologist would command a fabulous retainer fee to soothe my husband's ego and counsel my daughters.

I was full of new self-esteem when my husband arrived home from work. After all, my position in life commands top dollar.

"Honey," he said throwing his shirt on the bed, "will you remember to sew the button on my shirt when you wash it?"

"Sure," I told him. "That will be $3.20 plus tip."

"What are you talking about?" he asked.

I proudly pointed out the value of the work the average homemaker performs each week, telling him I was now worth $41,000 a year.

"Well, forget the button," he said. "I'll have the cleaners put it on. They're cheaper, and they always iron the shirts."

"I've been meaning to speak to you about the wash," I said, quickly seizing the opportunity. "I think I should be getting about $48 a week for washing clothes. And another $50 for folding the clothes and putting them away. And the occasional ironing amounts to about $25 a week."

My husband just laughed.

"Twenty-five dollars a week for ironing," he snickered. "Who are you kidding? I'll pay you $25 on the spot if you can even find the iron!"

I could see he wasn't so impressed with my new-found value. After dinner I tried some new tactics.

"If we had just eaten this meal in a restaurant," I said, "you would have paid the cook $3 to prepare the food. And you would have tipped the waitress $5 for serving you. And part of the bill would have gone to the dishwasher for cleaning all the pots and pans."

He just grinned. "If I were in a restaurant, I wouldn't have ordered tuna-noodle casserole. And if the kids at the next table were screaming like these kids, I would have left the restaurant. And if the waitress asked for a tip like you're doing, I would have left her empty-handed," he said.

Clearly we were getting nowhere.

"How much would I have to pay you to clean the toilet bowl," I snapped. "Or scrape the mold off the refrigerator shelves? Or clean the fingerprints off those sliding glass doors eight times a day?"

I pleaded with him to read the magazine article so he could see what I was talking about. It's not that I want to be paid $41,000 a year for taking care of the children and the house, I reasoned.

"That's good," he said, "because if you want $41,000 a year, you'll just have to find a new house to clean and a new family to take care of. You've become a bit over-priced!"

He thought for a minute and had another "brilliant" idea. "Or you could go out and get a full-time job," he said. "Then you could afford to give yourself a raise!"

With that, I threw the magazine in the garbage can. Those articles about liberated women have about as much lasting value as a TV anchorperson. Here today, gone tomorrow.

4
The trick is knowing when to get away

It's easy to tell when a mother needs a vacation.

The symptons are universal. They're instantly recognizable.

• If you go out to dinner with some friends, and you lean over and start cutting the meat on the plate next to you, never losing a beat in the conversation, it's time for vacation.

• If your dinner companion leaves the table and you tell him "Don't forget to wipe after you go to the potty," it's time for a vacation.

• If the conversation turns to literature and you start reviewing "Babar's Birthday Surprise" while everyone else is discussing "Cosmos" by Carl Sagan, it's time for a vacation.

• When you're out on the tennis courts and you notice that you've tied your own shoe laces in double knots, it's time for a vacation.

• If you're driving the car with an adult in the front seat and you put your arm out in front of her every time you step on the brake, it's time for a vacation.

• When you go to a restaurant for brunch and find you're ordering "eggy crackers" while everyone else at the table has ordered eggs benedict, it's time for a vacation.

- If you find yourself shouting **"PUNCH BUG!"** every time you spot a Volkswagen on the road it's time for a vacation.
- If you're so addicted to car-pooling that you get up, dress the kids, fill the lunch boxes and drive around the regular route, only to find out that it's Saturday morning, it's time for a vacation.

When all of these things happen in one week, you soon realize that there's no time to wait for vacation. To preserve what little sanity is left, it's imperative to take a weekend off from the kids — post haste!

When my husband came home from work and found me packing the suitcases, he immediately sensed trouble.

"We're going on a weekend vacation," I told him. "It's my treat. Diane has the kids until Sunday. Start packing!"

Planning a getaway is great fun, but when it comes time to actually say goodbye to the kids, it's all I can do not to cancel the reservations and stay home.

Once on the road, in a car that is unusually quiet, the freedom was refreshing. That feeling of freedom was short-lived, however. No matter how far you get away, I've learned, your kids are always with you.

Checking into a motel, my first inclination was to call home to make sure the kids were OK.

"I forgot to tell Diane about Beth's medicine," I explained to my husband. "And I want to be sure Andrea has her bathing suit."

He convinced me that the kids could get along for three days without my interference. But from that point on, every time I walked into the motel room, the first thing I looked at was the little red light on the telephone to make sure there weren't any messages about the children.

The first day away was tough. I was up at 7 a.m. and searching the motel room for the lunch boxes and book satchels.

A shopping excursion turned out to be a real fiasco. I found myself passing up Saks and Gucci, and heading instead for the toy stores and the children's departments.

"Which stuffed animal should I take back to the kids?" "If only Beth were here to try on these clothes." "I wonder if they'll like these souvenirs?"

The second day was easier. I woke up to the sound of silence rather than the noise of Saturday morning cartoons. We had a leisurely breakfast without having to worry about spilled orange juice and jelly stains on the carpet. But all the while I was thinking, "wouldn't the kids love to be here."

A tour Saturday afternoon turned out to be something "the kids would really enjoy." And in the back of my mind, I made plans to bring the kids over to see the attractions.

That night we had a romantic dinner by candlelight, but our conversation centered on the children.

"I hope the kids remembered to take their vitamins and brush their teeth," I told my husband. "I wonder if they got to bed on time." Talk about romantic dialogue!

Finally, after a few glasses of wine, I began to unwind and my guilt trip turned into my dream trip. For once, the kids didn't have the last word.

5
Who wrote 'wash me' on the bathroom mirror?

There are two types of people in this world.
One is the compulsive cleaner, who waxes the

toilet seat and can't live with fingerprints on the dining room table.

The second type of person is the casual cleaner. This person can ignore a crayon mark on the bathroom door and doesn't mind dust on the tops of picture frames.

Generally speaking, neither of these two types can live with the other. The compulsive cleaner considers the casual cleaner a slob, a mess-aholic. And the casual cleaner thinks of the compulsive cleaner as a fanatic.

For the sake of cleaner copy, let's call the compulsive cleaner **Type A**. The minute someone runs water in the sink of her house, she dashes in with a towel and wipes off the faucets so there won't be any water spots.

Let's call the casual cleaner **Type B**. If the minister is coming over for a visit, she'll fish the wet bathing suit out of the sink and drape it over the side of the tub.

For some unexplained reason, mothers usually seem to be **Type A** people and daughters tend to be **Type B**. I consider my mother to be a compulsive cleaner, and she thinks of me as, well, messy.

I think it's interesting, though, that my daughter regards me as a compulsive cleaner, and I refer to her as your basic slob.

Type A people live in a sterile world where kitchen counters never get dirty and pillow cases always smell fresh. They are able to catch dead leaves after they fall off a house plant and before they hit the carpet.

That carpet, by the way, is always perfectly plush, with never a footprint or a mark from the vacuum cleaner. Usually, it's some light color — often white.

You can tell that a **Type A** person lives in the house even before you walk inside. There are nev-

Who wrote 'wash me' on the bathroom mirror?

er any weeds in the garden out front, and the sidewalk sparkles in the sunshine.

Inside, there are never any fingerprints around the thermostat. Or on the light switches. Or on the windows.

If the **Type A** person happens to have kids — and it's doubtful — the toys are lined up side-by-side in the closet, underneath clothes that are neatly organized by color and size.

The kitchen is really the best sign of what type person you're dealing with. If the spices are lined up in alphabetical order in the cabinet, right away you know you're talking to a **Type A**. If recipes are neatly printed on cards and filed in a little card file, indexed of course, your friend is a compulsive, crazy-clean nut.

Type B's kitchen, however, is functional. Granted, there is dust on the top of the refrigerator, but who's tall enough to see it anyway?

There is a ketchup stain on the white telephone, and cookbooks are stacked in one corner with recipes (that have been torn from magazines) tucked in between pages. Clean glasses are emptied from the dishwasher when they're needed, not when the wash cycle is through.

Being honest with myself, I guess I'm a **Type B**. Looking around, the windows are so dirty I can hardly see out through the streaks of grape jelly. Cobwebs decorate the chandelier. It would take two coats of paint to cover up the dirt on the walls, but what can you expect with a toddler running around the house?

If company were coming for dinner tonight, it would take me 15 minutes to clean off the dining room table. And another 15 minutes to find some place to put all the stuff. You see, there's just no more room under my bed!

Even though I'm a **Type B** person, there's one thing that can thrust me into a **Type A** frenzy — an overnight visit by a **Type A** friend. That calls for a thorough housecleaning, which is a major undertaking in my world.

Dog bones come out from under the sofa and moldy tomatoes are removed from the far reaches of the refrigerator shelf. If necessary, I'll even polish the copper bottoms of my pots and pans, but I refuse to take an old toothbrush and shine up the monograms on the silver. I may be a fool, but I'm not a sadist!

Despite what my daughter thinks, I could never be a **Type A** person, at least not until she and her sister are off on their own and I no longer have to worry about orange juice dripping down the front of the refrigerator. Be honest, how many times have you had the carpet cleaned one day and the kids spill their milk the next?

But I guess I'll always consider my daughter a **Type B,** because behind every messy person is a meticulous mother. And that's the way it will always be. Right mom?

6
Tempers flare on our barbecue grill!

If I end up in divorce court, our barbecue grill will surely be Exhibit A when it comes time to list the evidence. Every time my husband lights up the barbecue, tempers at our house get hotter than the grill itself.

To me, there's nothing more pleasurable in life than a rare steak, cooked over charcoal. I repeat, nothing!

My husband has a difficult time accepting this attitude. He thinks I just like to avoid cooking meals or cleaning the oven. And there may be a little truth to that.

Our first grill was a hibachi. It was great for one steak or two hamburgers. But when we had company, I had to resort to the stove.

On our first anniversary, we bought one of those kettle-type grills, and we were in heaven. In no time my husband knew exactly how long to cook meat so that it was done to perfection.

But four years ago he came home with a new gas grill, and tempers have been flaring ever since.

I'm not sure just what the problem is. The grill is out in the pool area, just 15 steps away from the kitchen. It's not like the old days, when he had to tramp out through the snow to cook a steak in 25-degree weather.

If you ask me, he's just never mastered the technique of cooking on a gas grill. If you ask him . . . well, you'd better not ask him!

Right off the bat, there's the problem of timing. He thinks everything he cooks on the grill takes 20 minutes to cook. From a three-inch sirloin to a dozen hotdogs, everything takes 20 minutes.

That estimate is always fine when I start cooking the rice or noodles so they will be done at the same time the steak comes off the grill. But usually, after 20 minutes have passed and I'm ready to take the rice off the stove, the steak is still rare enough to walk away.

The reverse also happens with regularity. When the hamburgers are perfectly done, the vegetables that I'm cooking still have 10 minutes to go and the only thing that gets steamed is me!

But clearly the biggest gripe I have concerns burnt meat. My husband likes to light the gas, flip the steaks on the grill, and walk away. Sometimes he reads the paper, sometimes he starts pulling weeds, sometimes he plays with the kids.

I'm usually the one who spots the flames soaring up around the steaks, reaching for the sky.

"Quick," I shout, "The steaks are burning!"

I have this line down pat. That's because I use it every week.

Everyone comes running, and we start splashing handfuls of water from the pool into the flames. That's when I really feel like raking my husband over the coals. And he always senses my mood.

"What's the matter," he asks. "Don't you like a little chlorine flavoring on your steak?" he asks, trying to make light of the incident.

But as I stand at the kitchen counter, trying to slice the crust off my $14.95 steak, there is nothing that can brighten my mood. Then tempers start to simmer.

Tempers flare on our barbecue grill!

"Why can't you just stand there and watch the steak as it cooks so it won't burn?"

"Why should I stand around for 20 minutes watching a steak? I've got better things to do with my time. Why don't you just cook it yourself?"

"Why don't you just learn how to use the grill so I won't have to cook it myself?"

"Why don't you learn how to use the oven so I won't have to learn how to use the grill?"

"Why don't you just . . ."

Come to think of it, if we do end up in divorce court, I can't imagine who will get custody of the barbecue grill. Probably the children!

7
To love, honor, and take out the garbage

I have only one reservation about the Equal Rights Amendment. I'm afraid women will end up with the garbage duty. And that's one right I'm not too anxious to receive.

To love, honor, and take out the garbage

In our house, it's always been the man's job to take out the garbage. Call it sexist if you will, but that's the way it was in my parents' house, and in my grandparents' house, and on up the family tree. And that's the way I intend to keep it!

If God had intended for women to take out the garbage every night, we would have been born holding Glad Bags. As it is, it's bad enough being born with a scrub brush in one hand and a vacuum cleaner attachment in the other.

Taking out the garbage has always been something of a sore spot in our marriage.

My philosophy is simple: the garbage bag in the kitchen should be emptied every day. My husband, however, thinks the garbage bag should be emptied only when it is full.

Full is when the bag is overflowing with pork chop bones and moldy bread crusts, rotting orange peels and brown bananas, old newspapers and sour cream containers. Delicately balanced on top are several egg shells, a soup can full of coffee grounds, and an empty mayonnaise jar.

When the coffee grounds start to spill over onto the floor and there is just no room for the wad of paper towels, my husband finally gets the message. Swearing all the way out to the garbage can, he slams the door and mutters something about equal rights.

There are several variations to this scene.

1. When we bring home pizza and there is just no room for the large cardboard box, the garbage bag must be emptied immediately.

2. If I want the garbage carried out early, I can always fix fish for dinner. Even my husband can't stand the thought of fish decaying in our kitchen overnight.

3. When I get totally disgusted, I will usually start a second garbage bag going in the kitchen,

making it so difficult to move around that it is imperative for him to empty the first.

4. (The most fun to watch.) On occasion, the lid from a can in the garbage will slit the bag, causing the coffee grounds and the egg shells and the chicken bones to fall out through the bottom as my husband walks through the kitchen toward the garage.

Then the words start to fly faster than the garbage.

"How can you fill this bag so full?"

"Why don't you empty it more often?"

"Why don't **YOU** empty it some time?"

"That's not my job!"

"Well, what makes you think it's **MY** job?"

And so it goes. I was surprised the other day to see my husband gathering up a garbage bag that was only half full. Then I realized he was showing our older daughter how to twist the top closed and put it in the garbage can outside.

Later, I got her aside. Picking the sticky lid from a lemonade can off the floor and scraping up some peanut shells that had been scattered around the garbage bag, I tried to explain the facts of life.

"There's something you should know, and it's very important," I told her.

"Taking out the garbage is a man's job. It's his moral duty, no matter what they tell you in the women's liberation movement."

8
Surviving germ warfare

I could be on my death bed, and the rest of the family would want to know what's for dinner.

But let my husband get a little case of the sniffles, and everything at our house shuts down so we can all cater to his every whim.

I can't figure out why men, who pride themselves on being so virile and independent, become helpless babes when they get sick. But deep down inside, I suspect it has something to do with **MOTHER!**

Most men seem to take on childlike qualities when they get sick. They moan and fuss until they get the attention they deserve.

I've found the quickest solution to sickness in the male species is vast quantities of chicken noodle soup, just like mother used to make. In fact, that's usually the only thing my husband will eat when he comes down with the flu.

When a man gets sick, he doesn't stay in the bedroom all day. No way! If he stayed in the bedroom, the rest of the family might forget that he was sick.

The best place for a sick man to spend the day seems to be on the couch in the living room. That way everyone else in the family can tiptoe around him, trying in vain not to disturb him.

When my husband is feeling a bit under the weather, he doesn't miss a chance for everyone to administer to his every need.

From his vantage point on the sofa, he can see me folding three loads of wash, and he knows just the right point to ask for a Kleenex. Or two aspirin. And don't forget the glass of water . . . not too cold.

When I'm sick with the flu, the kids drag me out of bed to change the TV channel. If I need some cough medicine, my only choice is to drive to the

Surviving germ warfare

drugstore. I try to hide in the bedroom, but everyone knows where to find me.

At our house, the first sign of trouble is when my husband comes up to me and says "Do I have a fever?"

I get the old thermometer out and stick it under his tongue. Invariably he comes up with 98.9, and he starts asking for chicken noodle soup. And Saltines with butter spread on them.

At 98.9, he is too weak to get up out of bed to do anything but complain.

"All I want for lunch is some Jell-O," he'll say. "Cherry Jell-O."

If we don't have anything but strawberry Jell-O in the house, he says something like "That's OK, forget the Jell-O."

Great! A sick martyr!

"Don't we have anything to read?" he usually asks, trying to make his way to the sofa.

Never mind the fact that there are stacks of unread magazines and a dozen paperback books in the bedroom. He usually wants the latest copy of a magazine that is still on the newsstand.

With the sick husband in the living room, all the normal action in the house must take place somewhere else.

"Can't you kids play outside today?" he says in a feeble voice.

Despite the fact that he wants the kids outside, he wants me to sit beside him all day so I can hold his hand, or pat his head, or check for the 40th time to see if he still has a fever.

None of these new-fangled miracle drugs seems to work on my husband. Oh, no! He's thoroughly convinced that there's nothing in this world that can't be cured by either chicken noodle soup, witch hazel, or a hot water bottle.

37

I, on the other hand, am absolutely certain that the world's greatest cure-all is Vicks! Why, get me near a cough or a cold or a simple sore throat, and, like Superman, I race to the rescue. I've been known to smear Vicks on even the most casual of acquaintances.

And you wouldn't believe how fast it works. My husband, for example, can't stand the smell of Vicks. So when I think it's time for his little illness to be over, I just walk toward him with a big jar of Vicks. Instantly, he starts to feel better! Before I can get near him, he's on his feet again, making the bed and doing anything he can to avoid the Vicks.

And girls, there's one more magic quality about Vicks that you don't read about on the label but you might want to file in your memory bank. Vicks may not reduce a fever but it can cool your husband's ardor in a matter of seconds. If you want to ensure yourself of a good night's sleep, just slap on a little Vicks. It beats the heck out of a headache!

9
That must be someone else on my driver's license

If the driver's license bureau doesn't soon get a new photographer, I may have to resort to plastic surgery.

Surely I can't look as bad as my license claims! For the past four years I have shown my driver's license only under threat of arrest. And even then I slip on some dark glasses so the policeman can't see my embarrassment.

For some reason, when they issued me a license during my first week in Florida, I wasn't prepared to have that flash go off. The photograph was awful!

I took one look at my new license and told the clerks, "This can't be mine. There's been some mistake."

They just laughed.

After having spent days studying all those silly rules of the road in that little book, how was I to know a picture-taking session would accompany the final exam?

"Why didn't you tell me," I asked the clerk, an obvious sadist.

"They should print it right here on the front page," I yelled, shoving that little book under her nose. "Rule number one should be to visit the beauty parlor before taking the test!"

Her only attempt at comforting me was just more cruelty.

"Maybe you'll get a better photo next time."

How was I to know that the "next time" was to be four years later. That was a long four years!

In desperation, I tried to avoid any activity that required some form of identification, and that's not easy.

That must be someone else on my driver's license

Whenever I had to cash a check at the grocery store, I would wait in line where the clerk knew me so I wouldn't have to show my license. I took to driving slowly so I wouldn't get stopped by police.

And I buried my license carefully behind my Social Security card in my wallet, so that in case someone happened to get inside my purse they wouldn't see the awful truth.

The four years seemed like an eternity. Every time my birthday rolled around, I would keep checking the mails to see if a new license application had arrived from the state.

Then finally the day arrived. It was time for a new driver's license.

Of course I studied the rules again, memorizing all the road signs and learning when to pass on a two-lane road. But more importantly, I went on a two-week crash diet, I got my hair done, I put on the old makeup, and I tried to pull myself together as best I could.

After donning my nicest outfit, I drove to the license testing center, completed the questions, turned in my test, and prepared for **THE MOMENT**.

"Go over there and sit on that bench," the clerk at the license bureau told me after checking my test score.

I sat down, looked at the camera lens, and smiled my best Ultra-Brite smile. Then I noticed something new.

There was a sign beside the camera. I leaned my head forward, scrunched up my nose, squinted my eyes, and read "If your photo doesn't turn out, don't blame the photographer."

Just as I was reading the word "blame," the flash went off, and the camera caught me at the worst possible moment.

41

I knew, even before I saw the results, that I was in for another humiliating four years.

The bright flash made my blond hair look white. The glasses sliding down my nose made me look like I've barely survived middle age. And the startled expression on my face told the whole story.

"Here," I yelled, standing up. "Don't just stop at my face! Why don't you take a picture of my fat thighs while you're at it? If you want to torment me, why not get a profile?"

Obviously the people in the driver's license bureau are used to hysterical women.

"Maybe you'll get a better photo the next time," the clerk said, steering me to the door so I wouldn't agitate the rest of the crowd.

Well, I spent weeks in severe depression. I thought about burning my license as a protest. I thought about cutting it up in little pieces and mailing it back to the state. I even contemplated giving up driving so I wouldn't have to face the ordeal every few years.

The whole messy incident ruined my birthday. Even now I have trouble writing about it.

But last week my husband came home sporting his new driver's license.

"Take a look at this," he said smugly, pointing to a photograph that made him look like Robert Redford. I just don't know how he gets those license bureau photographers to make him look younger after four years, while my license photo looks like I just missed the best years of my life.

So now, my husband is the one hiding his license. That's because he knows that if I find it, I'm going to cut it up in little pieces and send it back.

That's the only way I'll get any satisfaction for the next four years.

10
My balance of payments is a credit to MasterCard

If I knew 15 years ago that my MasterCard balance was going to be so high, I would have studied law or medicine in college rather than journalism.

Let's face it, you need more than an education to survive today — you need credit!

Every so often someone comes up to me at a party and says "You're so lucky to be able to write for a living. I get so much enjoyment out of your articles."

That's great for the old ego, but on the whole, I'd rather be taking out someone's appendix instead of sitting at this typewriter. After all, when was the last time you heard your doctor complain about his MasterCard balance. He probably pays the bill in full each month.

And did you ever see an attorney wait while the department store clerk calls up the credit office to check his account? Cool as a cucumber, I'll bet.

It's not that attorneys have nerves of steel. It's simply that they know their credit rating is impeccable.

I, on the other hand, sweat buckets while that clerk is on the phone. In case the news from the credit office is bad, I always want to be able to make a quick exit.

I don't want to mislead you. Money isn't everything to me. But a little extra cold cash would relieve the balance of payments somewhat.

My friend Estelle summed it up the other day. Estelle is in real estate, and we were on the way to her bank to cash one of her commission checks. When I found out that she made more by selling one house than I made in the entire year, I started clawing the seat covers of her new Cadillac.

"Face it, honey," she said. "You just picked the wrong profession. The arts is as bad as being a volunteer."

She's rotten, but she's right. You've probably known at least a dozen "poor starving artists" in your lifetime, but have you ever once met a "poor starving physician?"

It doesn't take long to realize that the electric company isn't interested in the fact that six magazines have rejected your last piece of work. All they care about is that monthly check that hasn't arrived. The electric company may support the arts, but it doesn't plan to carry artists!

In those pre-inflation days, things weren't quite as bad. Frankly, my husband used to encourage my literary efforts simply because he could use my expenses as a tax write-off. Those were the good old days when he would realize my true value every April 15.

But when toilet paper started costing 40 cents a roll and peanut butter hit $2 a jar, those days were over.

After talking to Estelle, I was determined to teach my children the facts about the fight for economic survival. I stopped at the toy store on the way home and bought a doctor's kit for my youngest daughter, and a plumber's kit for my oldest.

I figure that my daughter the plumber can help

My balance of payments is a credit to MasterCard

pay the cost of medical school for my daughter the doctor. That way I won't have to add the tuition to my MasterCard account.

And maybe, by the time I die, my balance of payments will come out even.

11
Some day my prints will come

My 9-year-old daughter got a camera for her birthday, and it's been like Candid Camera around our house ever since.

Wherever you are, whatever you're doing, there's a good chance she'll capture you on film... when you least expect it!

Click! Flash! There's Aunt Louise putting in her dentures.

My daughter has been waiting for this camera for more than a year. It's the one thing she has asked for constantly. Now that she has it, she isn't wasting any time making up for lost photos.

Click! Flash! There's mom cleaning the toilet bowl.

Click! Flash! There's mom cleaning the toilet bowl again, only this time her facial expression is a bit more contorted.

My daughter has a tendency to take more than one shot of the same scene, even if it doesn't merit even one shot. The camera has an automatic wind, so I'm not sure if her finger is working faster than her brain, or if she's just so excited to be able to take photos that she goes overboard.

Whatever the reason, she went through the first roll of film in 20 minutes on her birthday and then begged for more film.

Click! Flash! There's her dad swearing at the puppy.

Some day my prints will come!

Click! Flash! There's her dad swearing at the photographer.

We've tried to tell her to save film for better photos. But trying to tell a young lady how to do anything is difficult at best.

Click! Flash! There's her sister reaching into the peanut butter jar.

Frankly, there's very little privacy at our house with the mad photographer running around. You just can't get away with anything anymore.

Click! Flash! There she is holding the camera in front of her face, taking a picture of herself.

Click! Flash! Now she's taking a photo of the Lite-Brite picture she and her sister have just made.

Click! Flash! She just took a photograph of a butterfly seconds after it had flown away.

She's been warned that it's very expensive to get film developed. And she knows she will have to pay the bill herself. But that still doesn't inhibit her desire to take photos of everyone and everything.

Click! Flash! She just took a picture of her teeth.

Despite all my efforts to maintain a sense of calm, I came completely unglued.

"Why did you waste the film on your teeth," I shouted.

"It's simple, Mother," she replied in that sassy tone only a 9-year-old can achieve. "I'm going to send this film to the dentist. That way he won't have to X-ray my teeth this year."

Click! Flash! There's mom looking at the prints from the first roll of film.

Thank heavens Aunt Louise was out of focus. All you can see is a set of dentures.

There's a photo of someone cleaning a toilet bowl, but we'll never know who. The head is missing.

Middle Age & Other Spreads

The picture of dad swearing at the photographer was taken a bit too close. It should be the photo we send to the dentist to see if his teeth are still in good shape.

That photo of sister reaching into the jar of peanut butter came out as a great head shot. You can't even see her arms.

And the self-portrait. Well, all I can say is that's the most beautiful sky I've ever seen.

I guess the whole family is going to be starring in Candid Camera for a while. At least as long as my daughter's money holds out.

After that, we'll just have to see what develops.

12
Kids think a car is a wastebasket with wheels

The way I see it, you have a choice in life.

You can have a nice car with light blue velour

Kids think a car is a wastebasket with wheels

upholstery, or you can have kids. Don't ever presume you can have both.

I love my kids. I love my car. Unfortunately, my kids think of my car as a wastebasket with wheels. Thank goodness I'll never hear what my car thinks of my kids.

The first sign of touble came shortly after we got our car. We were riding home from school one day and got stuck behind a truck.

My daughter took one whiff of the exhaust fumes and promptly threw up all over the floor, missing only the rubber floor mats. It just so happens that the carpet on the floor of the car is also light blue. Well, it was light blue. Now the color resembles the parking lot at the mall.

I don't know why any car manufacturer would be so bold as to put light blue plush carpet in any car. Not even Nancy Reagan has shoes with clean bottoms.

Another problem with light blue velour upholstery soon became apparent.

You should never stop at a drive-in bank teller. They always give the kids a lollypop — you know, the bright red ones that drip when they're wet.

"Why don't you kids look at what you're doing?" I asked my daughters the other day as I was trying to scrape the chewing gum off the back seat.

"I don't know where it came from," my oldest daughter said, looking with suspicion at her younger sister.

"I didn't do it! It was her," the little one started to scream.

I knew it was a no-win proposition.

Kids have no appreciation for something as big as an automobile. All they know is that it takes them to school and it's a place to dump trash.

You can always tell which cars belong to adults with children. They're the ones with the melted crayons on the rear window. When the driver opens the car door and six candy wrappers, two suckers, a shredded Kleenex and a stick of gum fall out, you know that motorist is a parent.

To kids, every receptacle is a place to store things. The ashtray in our car is so full of chewing gum wrappers that there's not even room for a used match. The little holes in the armrests are overflowing with bubble gum, erasers, toy cars and other important treasures.

There are footprints on the ceiling, on the doors, on the roof, on the hood and on the windshield. It looks as if our car was the one used by the 27 clowns in the circus who pile out, one after the other.

And under the seat . . . oh, under the seat! Under the seat are things you don't dare think about. A half-eaten Big Mac, a chocolate-covered straw, an Easter egg, some seashells from last month's trip to the beach, and some Silly Putty. I keep expecting to see a turtle crawl out from under the front seat any day now.

Auto companies don't warn you that children and velour don't mix. In fact, every time I see that car ad with that elegantly dressed little girl sitting quietly on the front seat of her father's luxury car, I laugh to myself. Just where do you rent children like that anyway?

I've decided that my next car is going to be childproofed. No more velour seatcovers. It's going to be vinyl, covered with plastic. No more plush carpeting. It's going to be linoleum — the no-wax kind. And there will be little garbage cans in each door that can be emptied at the touch of a button.

And what am I going to call this new innovation in automobiles? Why, the Spock-mobile, of course!

13
Who ever called summer a vacation?

If you ask me, there's no sweeter sound in all the world than the sound of school bells ringing in the end of summer.

Let's face it, the summer is the pits if you're a mother. I have enough togetherness in the three months of summer to last me for the rest of the year. Summer always starts out great. There is the thrill of sleeping until 10 in the morning. There are the carefree hours at the beach or the pool. There is the joy of getting reacquainted with your kids.

Yes, that first day is great. But then there's the second day. You wake up to the sound of Fred Rogers on the television set and you know it's going to be a long summer.

"Why don't you kids turn that television off and go outside and play," I say, propping open my bleary eyes and forcing a smile.

"There's nothing to do," my children reply.

That always wakes me up.

"Nothing to do!" I shout. "You could clean up your room! You could throw away that junk in your closet! You could vacuum the rug! You could polish the table! What do you mean there's nothing to do?"

"Oh, Motherrr..."

At least that technique always gets them out of the house.

Summer vacation for the kids is great. But for mothers, it's a different story. Those lazy, crazy days of summer are anything but lazy. They are, however, definitely crazy!

"Just how many days is it until you go back to school," I ask my daughters as casually as possible every Aug. 1.

They never have any idea. They're oblivious to everything but the pool, the bikes and the roller skates. For them, school is a million thoughts away.

"Gee, won't it be fun to get back to the classroom," I asked my oldest daughter during the second week of August. I was preoccupied with picking no less than 500 sandburs from her jeans before they went into the washing machine.

"I bet you're anxious to see all your school friends from last year," I told her early in the third week of August as I scraped the mud off her once-white tennis shoes and tried to find a shoelace to replace the broken one.

"Aren't you at least a little excited about going into a new grade," I asked her as I scrubbed little footprints off the kitchen floor for the fourth time that morning.

The way I look at it, when school's in session, you have enough clean glasses to last for the entire day. Clothes don't get nearly so dirty. Neither does the carpet.

Take the glasses, for instance. For some reason, during the summer kids think my kitchen is just one big spigot. Every 10 minutes a little head pops in the doorway and says, "Can I have a drink?" I can't get past 11 a.m. without going through every clean glass in the house.

And kids bring home the strangest pets during their summer vacations. Things like turtles, and

Who ever called summer a vacation?

crabs, and lizards, and cats, and caterpillars, and the list goes on and on.

Once kids are back in school, my house starts to take on some semblance of order. There's only one pitcher of Kool-Aid in the refrigerator rather than four pitchers in various hues. And at last I can get rid of those awful trays of frozen lemonade that have spilled all over the inside of the freezer all summer long.

But best of all is the peace and quiet. I don't have to lock myself in the bathroom to get away. You can't imagine how many hours I spend in the bathroom during the summer.

Of course, you can't let the kids think you're really ecstatic seeing them head off for school once again. You've got to show some remorse over losing them each fall.

I usually turn to my old child psychology technique in dealing with the situation.

"I know you're happy at the thought of seeing all your school friends again," I told my daughters. "But I sure will miss those happy times we shared this past summer."

My older daughter looked up at me in surprise, full of concern at the thought of leaving me home alone.

"What will you do all day, Mother?"

I assured her that I had plenty of things to keep me occupied.

"Yeah, she gets to watch Fred Rogers while we have to go to school," my younger daughter chimed in.

"Somehow, Fred just isn't the same without you around," I smiled. That old child psychology works every time!

14
Over-sleeping can be alarming

Why is it that kids wake up at the crack of dawn on Saturday and Sunday, but when Monday morning rolls around, you can't even drag them out of bed?

Could it be that television set in our family room? And those cartoons that evidently start at 6 a.m. each Saturday and conclude at noon on Sunday? It must be. I can't figure out any other answer.

For some reason my kids are attracted to those Saturday morning specials, and nothing I can say seems to discourage their viewing. They never miss a show.

But come Monday morning and school time, I can't get them out of bed for anything in the world.

Every weekday it's the same story.

"Come on, kids. It's time to get up. Come on, kids, you better get up! Come on, kids, wake up and get out of bed. **COME ON, KIDS!**"

I prop my nine-year-old daughter up in bed and struggle to get clothes on her limp body. I drag her to the table and force food into her mouth. I scrub her teeth and comb her hair. I pack her lunch and shove her out the door, praying that she somehow makes it to school each day.

"This morning routine is driving me crazy," I told my friend Hortense last month. "If I didn't pick my daughter up out of bed and force her out

Over-sleeping can be alarming

the door, she'd spend the whole week in bed asleep! No matter how much I nag and threaten, she won't get up in the mornings."

Hortense told me I was going about it in the wrong way.

"Give her an alarm clock and tell her she's responsible for herself," Hortense said.

The logic was frighteningly simple.

"I couldn't take the chance," I said. "She'd flunk the third grade for sure!"

But deep inside I knew Hortense was right. It was time for my daughter to decide for herself whether she was going to get up on Monday morning.

I took my daughter out that afternoon to buy an alarm clock.

"Why are we doing this?" she asked me.

I tried to explain that she was going to be responsible for getting up, getting dressed, fed and out the door from now on.

"Mother, that's ridiculous!" was her only comment.

Sure enough, it was. I found myself the next morning standing at her door, waiting for the alarm to go off. And when it did, I found myself waiting for her to reach over, turn it off, get out of bed with a smile, and ask "What's for breakfast?"

It took all the force I could muster not to go in and turn off the alarm. Five minutes later, there was movement in the bed. Then a little hand pushed the alarm clock to the floor. And then I heard myself say "Come on, it's time to get up!" That's when I bit my tongue and realized that I had a real problem!

That night I set up some ground rules.

"If you stay in bed too long, you'll miss breakfast. And you'll be pretty hungry during your morning classes.

"If you don't get up in time to make it to school, you'll have to explain to your teacher why you're late. I'm not going to do it. It's your responsibility. "You're the one who has to make the decisions."

Easier said than done, I might add. When you've been making the decisions for your child for nine years, it's hard to let go in one day.

But miraculously, my daughter caught on quicker than I did. Lately I've been waking up to find her dressed and waiting for breakfast in the mornings.

Last weekend, I was trying to catch a few extra winks of sleep on Saturday morning when I was rudely awakened by my daughter.

"How come you're up at the crack of dawn every weekday morning, but I can't drag you out of bed on Saturday?" she asked with a smile. I threw the alarm clock at her and went back to sleep. These kids today are just too smart!

15
The way we were

When your child asks you what black-and-white television is, you know you've entered middle age.

Yes, it's true. My 9-year-old daughter overheard a conversation about old black-and-white TV shows the other day.

"What's black-and-white mean, Mom?" she asked.

That casual little remark, and an article I read the other day about nostalgia, led me into the full realization that I am no longer on the borderline of middle age. I'm there!

For instance, how many of you remember curb feelers? For all you kiddies of the Brooke Shields generation, we're not talking about lustful derelicts.

Curb feelers were those little wires that went "ping" when they touched the curb. I think their sole function was to protect white sidewalls.

They came just after running boards disappeared and just before Brillo became so popular.

The disappearance of curb feelers means one of two things. Americans are becoming more adept at parallel parking, or people just don't care what their white sidewalls look like. I, for one, am no better at parallel parking than I was 20 years ago when I was learning how to drive.

The little wooden clothespin has also gone the way of curb feelers. I'm not talking about the clip kind. I'm referring to the clothespin with the little round head at one end and the two prongs that made perfect legs for a doll. A little paint or nail polish, a piece of gingham and a ribbon was all it took to turn that clothespin into a Martha Washington doll.

And how many of you remember the oleomargarine that came with its own little capsule of red dye? I remember mashing that dye into the margarine. I guess it was to make it look more like butter.

While we're on the subject, when milk used to come in glass bottles, there was that delicious little layer of cream on the top. And the funny little foil cap that covered the bottle. Not to mention the milkman who delivered. I guess all of that has gone the way of house calls by doctors.

How about wallpaper cleaner? When I was a kid, that glob of wallpaper cleaner was more fun than modeling clay. Maybe Silly Putty just forced it into oblivion.

There was a time when every grocery store had a machine that ground fresh coffee while you waited. Oh, the aroma!

And my children find it hard to believe that when I was a child, my grandmother could actually call up the grocery store and have the items delivered.

Does anyone still have a hot-water bottle? Or a little blue eye-bath cup? Or a down-filled comforter?

When was the last time you saw one of those clocks shaped like a cat, with eyes that moved back and forth, and a tail that ticked off the seconds? Usually those clocks were right above the icebox, which didn't even remotely resemble today's refrigerator.

I know my mother must have a drawer full of little white gloves, but I haven't seen them on

The way we were

anyone for quite a while. Those gloves must be stored right next to some crinolines and hoop skirts, perhaps in a box under a stack of pillbox hats.

Do you still have any 78 rpm records left in your collection? For that matter, is 78 still a choice on today's record players, or is it simply 33 and 45?

Remember the washing machine with the swing-away ringer? My grandmother was so proud of that, but I was terrified.

And speaking of some good recollections, remember player pianos, pop beads, Fuller Brush men, cast iron skillets, charm bracelets, 3-D movies and high-topped sneakers?

Sooner or later, there will come a time when nobody remembers the little vent window that used to air out the car so well, or stand-up radios that were actually a piece of furniture.

Everybody has the great capacity to forget the bad and remember the good. And that's why it's so wonderful to remember when . . .

16
Don't all shirts come with ring around the collar?

I think the people in this nation who are planning to boycott television programming are fighting for the wrong cause.

To me, the sex and violence that appear on the television screens every night aren't nearly as offensive as the misleading and objectionable commercials that bombard us every day.

Frankly, by the time children are able to comprehend what's happening on the television screen, they are accustomed to violence. They've heard stories about cradles falling from tree boughs and Humpty Dumpty's shattering experience. And you can't convince me that Jack and Jill falling down the hill is a pretty sight!

It seems to me that the story about the old woman who lived in a shoe and had so many children she didn't know what to do says more about sex and violence than 10 episodes of Charlie's Angels!

What I find truly objectionable is the advertisement that leads my husband to believe it really is possible to get that dirty ring out of his collar. A husband shouldn't have that kind of knowledge. It just leads to frustration and disappointment. It should lead to the dry cleaners!

Husbands, by the way, have special roles in commercials. Everything seems to center around

Don't all shirts come with ring around the collar?

the man. The man must have clean shirts, socks with no lint, jeans with no grease stains, and soap that leaves him refreshed and smelling good. In fact the only problem men seem to have in commercials is getting a close clean shave and picking out the right deodorant.

I guess there are some men on the TV advertisements who do have other problems. There's the businessman whose chief concern is getting a message to the other side of the country overnight. Fortunately, he doesn't have to use the post office. And of course there is that man who is always losing his travelers checks, but that usually is no problem.

There's no denying it, the men have it knocked. But that's because the women in commercials are always cheerful and pleasant.

"You got grease from the car all over my new white towels? No problem! I'll just spray them with this special stain remover." You call that reality?

The mother in commercials is always depicted as a saintly person who can solve any little problem, never losing her smile and her sense of humor. Now just when was the last time you saw a real-life mother who smiled and had a sense of humor?

When children watch television, they expect mother to simply shrug her shoulders and get out a bottle of Handy Andy after the dog throws up on the freshly cleaned kitchen floor. A child who has been raised on a steady diet of television is shocked when he hears the words that are really directed at the dog.

My daughter thinks there really is a little man sailing in a little boat who lives inside our toilet tank. Now I ask you, which is worse, "Three's

Company" or one of the Marx brothers in our toilet bowl?

Is it fair to make children think there are mothers who actually iron their pillow cases, or make homemade strawberry ice cream, or go on camping trips?

Don't all shirts come with ring around the collar?

Do you want your child to grow up thinking there really is a deodorant that will keep you dry for two days, even in the Florida heat? Isn't it better that the kids learn to cope with wet shirts under their arms?

How many times have you seen a commercial showing a family seated around a large table waiting for mother to serve breakfast? The last time my family got together for breakfast was in February, 1978.

If my daughter started sitting around listening to her cereal snap and crackle, I'd begin to worry.

Just once I'd like to see some realism in television commercials. Kids would spill their milk and parents would scream in frustration. Fathers would drive old cars with bald tires and rusted fenders. Mothers would open the door to the dryer and break into tears at the thought of folding another load of clothes.

Dinner would be served on chipped plates, and the Mickey Mouse glasses would have that familiar dull film that I can't get rid of. Table talk would focus on keeping all four legs of the chair on the floor and not chewing with your mouth open rather than the merits of real butter versus the other spread.

And after dinner, everyone would bolt as quickly as possible to avoid getting stuck with the dishes, no matter what detergent was being used.

Mothers would appear in holey bathrobes rather than in those fancy hostess gowns. They would have their hair up in rollers, with bobby pins falling out onto the stove. They wouldn't wear makeup at 7 a.m., and wouldn't be able to remember where they put the lunchbox they had packed the night before.

Yes, once the majority of commercials are more moral, I'll start believing in the power of protest.

But until then, I'll just have to go along with that woman with arthritis who is able to hold up a skillet after taking some marvelous pain-relieving pill.

Television commercials are a pain in the neck, and the only relief in sight is to take two aspirin and laugh a lot.

17
Watching the best years of our lives

I'm sure that somewhere in America there must be a family that doesn't own a television set. But I can't imagine how they survive.

If lightning were to strike my television set tomorrow (God forbid), there is no doubt in my mind that my family would disregard the message from on high. They would rush out and buy a new TV.

Watching the best years of our lives

I used to worry about my children's obsession with television. But that was before I knew the facts.

A recent Roper poll says that Americans get more personal satisfaction from watching television than from anything else in their lives except their families.

And I thought I had it bad!

That's not all. In another national poll, more than 36 percent of the people surveyed said that the television set was one of their three most important household possessions.

Those are some sobering statistics. Let's all turn the TV volume down and reflect on them for a few seconds.

America is hooked on TV. My children are evidently no different than your children, no matter what their age.

On a typical Saturday night, one out of every two Americans is watching TV. The average household focuses on the TV tube for 43 hours and 52 minutes a week.

That's incredible! The great American pastime is TV, and we can't live without it.

"This has got to stop," I told my kids, punching the off button of the TV set just as the Dukes of Hazzard were about to wreck their car for the third time in 40 minutes.

"From now on," I said, adjusting my voice from a yell to a quieter decibel, "we aren't going to watch so much TV."

The silence was deafening. Finally my older daughter said, "I think she means it. We're in trouble!"

Then there was protest. Lots and lots of protest.

"But Barbara Mandrell is on tomorrow! You know that's my favorite show!"

"Mother, I can't live without seeing the Muppets this weekend."

"Why can't I just watch Sesame Street?"

"And The Cat from Outer Space is on HBO next week. You promised we could watch it!"

I was firm. No TV for a week. We were going to learn to live without that infernal boob tube.

My daughters looked at me as if they were about to collaborate on another version of "Mommie Dearest," but I held my ground.

"Then what are we going to do?" the kids asked.

My mind raced as I tried to find some attactive alternatives. Frankly, the thought of leading a family of four in conversation for a week sent chills up and down my spine.

"Well, there's reading," I started. "You both have hundreds of books to read."

"And you can listen to the radio. When I was a kid, we used to listen to shows like Fibber McGee and Molly, and the Lone Ranger," I said.

That was a mistake. I searched the dial for something stimulating, but my kids just aren't into the splendor of Bach, and I wasn't about to give in to the sound of punk rock.

Scrabble was good for two nights, but trying to find a game that is interesting for both adults and children is a losing battle. You can only play "Candyland" so many times before you start to scream.

"Invite some friends over," I told my daughter one afternoon. "We can enjoy spending the evening with friends."

She made a few phone calls and then looked up with that dejected expression. "They won't come over since we can't watch TV," she said.

As the week went by, I noticed my children reading more. They again started to communicate with each other. What worried me, however, was the fact that they were mainly reading TV Guide, and they were talking about the shows they were going to watch once our awful test-pattern life was over.

"Have you learned anything from this," I asked my kids after the week was up.

My younger daughter didn't waste any time. "I learned that I've got mean parents," she said.

I should have expected as much.

My nine-year-old thought a little bit before answering, leading me to believe that it was all worth it.

"I learned one thing," she said, leading me on. "I'm glad I didn't grow up when there wasn't any TV."

She reached over and pulled the button out, breaking a marvelous week-long silence. Bo and Luke were being chased by Boss Hogg on the Dukes of Hazzard, and I realized things hadn't changed at all.

We are a mobile society, frequently breaking our ties with past places and friends. Maybe that's why television is so important in our lives. The characters become our friends because they're dependable. They're there every week.

Still, it's hard to imagine that so many people get so much personal satisfaction out of watching things like Fantasy Island or Family Feud.

If television is man's best friend, I think we're all in the doghouse.

18
The vicious red fingernail set

Whatever happened to backgammon?

Remember those nostalgic days of yesteryear when a costly, classy backgammon set was as vital to the international jet-setter as his Gucci shoes, his Cartier watch and his Louis Vuitton luggage?

Why back then, not having a backgammon set was almost as gauche as having dandruff or ring-around-the-collar. I mean, it just wasn't done.

Everybody who was **ANYBODY** played backgammon . . . in the car, at the bar — even in the boudoir!

For some, backgammon in bed became a fashionable method of birth control. After all, it's hard to get in the mood for other things after your spouse just beat the pants off you . . . at backgammon, that is.

For others, backgammon became a socially acceptable way to pick up an easy date:

"Hi! What's your sign? Do you play backgammon? Your place or mine?"

Magazines and catalogues were filled with it.

Women's Wear Daily featured Jackie O playing backgammon in her jeans, Town and Country showed Princess Grace playing backgammon in her palace, and Cosmopolitan showed Burt Reynolds playing other things in his bedroom with backgammon in the backgound.

The vicious red fingernail set

On the streets there were as many backgammon sets as attache cases and they came in handsome leather for men and lovely Ultrasuede for the ladies.

Prices ranged anywhere from $5 for a cardboard and plastic model like mine to $5,000 for a set of jade markers on an alabaster board. The more expensive the set, the more status you were assured.

It was kind of like the chess craze that came and went in a fury a few years ago. Come on. Admit it. How many of you knew people who had gorgeous sets displayed in their living room or family room but had absolutely no idea how to play chess?

For a while there I was afraid that chess and backgammon might make that marvelous game of bridge as passe as dominoes or cribbage. But I had forgotten to take into account the drive and determination of those fanatic bridge players that I like to call "the vicious red fingernail set." Those broads wouldn't dream of letting bridge go down the tubes.

Devotees of backgammon play for relaxation and fun.

Bridge players play for blood!

While your skill at backgammon largely depends on how good you are at rolling doubles on a pair of dice, to be good at bridge you either have to have a mind like a computer or else be endowed with strong psychic powers of mental telepathy.

When I was growing up the vicious red fingernail set used to meet at our house regularly.

These gals took their bridge seriously and heaven help a last-minute substitute who announced she just plays bridge "for fun."

When the cards were good these bridge partners would be the best of friends, but let the tables turn and the luck change and pretty soon darts could be seen flying across the table!

Middle Age & Other Spreads

"What do you mean you weren't playing a short club?"

"How could you take me to five clubs with only three points in your hand?"

"That **WAS** a demand bid according to all the books I've read!"

But if you think bridge can be treacherous among friends, it's downright deadly for married couples.

For some reason I've never completely understood, you can play bridge with five other couples and play brilliantly with every other person in the room.

But just get teamed up with your spouse and watch out — all hell breaks loose!

"Just what were you doubling on?"

"Why can't you learn when to stop bidding?"

The vicious red fingernail set

I swear bridge can bring on a divorce as quickly as adultery.

And while bridge gives you every opportunity to display your wit and cunning, bridge clubs are also a perfect excuse for social one-upmanship.

If Bunny hosts bridge the first week and serves potato chips and pretzels, then it's only natural for Buffy to upstage her a little bit by serving cheese and crackers, vegetables and dip, and mixed nuts.

Kiki's not about to be outdone so the following week when it's her turn, she serves crackers with cream cheese and caviar and her special crab dip. Next Muffy decides a nice Salad Nicoise is in order, followed by homemade angel food cake, and by the time it gets back to Bunny again she's so nervous about what to serve that she calls in sick!

I guess when you come right down to it, the games people play are never quite as interesting as the people who play the games.

19
Table-top psychology: a lesson in good taste

What's on your coffee table?

An ebony backgammon set? Some Steuben glass animals? A collection of Meissen porcelain? An autogaphed copy of something deep? Or a sticky ring of spilled apple juice?

I've heard psychologists claim that the objects (or lack of) on the coffee table in your living room reveal a lot about your personality.

For instance, some people put games or adult toys out on display. That's an indication that the person is fun-loving.

Plants and flower displays show a love of nature. One of my friends has a huge fern in the middle of her coffee table — not because she is a nature lover but simply because she doesn't have anything else to put on display.

Prestigious books and magazines, carefully displayed but never really read, are a sign that the person is trying to impress guests.

My friend Hortense could be a case study for any psychologist trying to write a text book on coffee-table analysis.

The first time I visited Hortense's home, there was a beautiful art book open on the table in front of her new sofa. I glanced through the pretty pictures and put the closed book down, much to her dismay.

Table-top psychology: a lesson in good taste

"Don't close that book," Hortense shouted, her face pale. "My decorator told me to leave it open to page 75 so that it will look like I casually laid it on the table."

I couldn't believe what I was hearing.

I asked her why page 75.

"The colors on that page go so beautifully with my new sofa," she said without a smile. "And besides, the artist on that page is very 'in.'"

That same book was on her table for nearly a year, until she got a new decorator. And I don't mind telling you, by that time the colors on page 75 had faded more than her sofa.

Her new decorator thought Royal Copenhagen figurines were more suited to Hortense's coffee table.

"How do you keep them from getting broken?" I said one day as I stood between my little daughter and Hortense's coffee table, never taking my eyes off her fast little hands.

Hortense didn't seen concerned. Her decorator could always get more. I think he must have been in the importing business on the side.

Then one day I stopped at her house and there was an antique Mah-Jongg set sitting on the top of her coffee table.

"I didn't know you played Mah-Jongg," I said.

"I don't," Hortense replied. "I saw it on display at a model home, and it looked so nice I bought it on the spot. Do you think it makes me look more like a fun-loving person?"

When Hortense comes to my house, I usually entertain her out on the patio so she won't see my coffee table. The only thing on it is dust — and maybe a few fingerprints.

My one and only Royal Copenhagen figurine is safely up on the top shelf on my china cabinet, and my Ethan Allen catalog is the closest thing I have to an art book. The only games that ever grace my coffee table are all made by Fisher-Price, and I try to clear them off the table when the doorbell rings.

If I ever want to impress someone, I can always put out my Bloomingdale's catalog. Of course, it's got crayon marks on nearly every page, but people should be able to overlook that.

If psychologists think that a bare coffee table indicates a person is extremely neat, they're in for a surprise. In my house it simply means there is a little toddler running around, and anything left on the coffee table becomes hers. She just hasn't learned to appreciate good art or fine porcelain yet.

But I'll always remember what they keep telling Charlie the Tuna on television each week: "It's not good taste that counts, but what tastes good." And I've got to admit that while my coffee table doesn't exude good taste, the spilled apple juice should make it taste good.

20
There's nothing wrong with being stacked

One topic those fancy interior decorating magazines never seem to deal with is organization of your basic junk.

Just what do you do with the box full of canceled checks from 1969, or the Instamatic photos of your grandmother's 70th birthday party?

If you're anything at all like me, you just can't part with those old National Geographics, or the 1978 Neiman-Marcus Christmas catalog, or the picture your 9-year-old daughter drew for you when she was 5.

But just where do you put all these treasures?

My closets barely have enough room for the clothes, let alone boxes of goodies from the past. The areas under all of the beds in the house are already taken. The garage is packed, and the last time my husband went up in the attic, I didn't see him for three days.

My kitchen looks like the basement of an old 5-and-10¢ store. All available counter space is filled with items that don't seem to fit anywhere else.

Once somebody picks the last orange out of the fruit bowl, the dish mysteriously fills up with key chains, erasers, broken pencils, paper clips, assorted nuts and bolts, bubble gum wrappers, and anything else that doesn't have a home.

I don't know why, but the dining room table has become a convenient place to drop the mail, the newspaper, those special reports my husband always intends to read but never gets around to, and other items "too important to lose."

The only way to keep the table clean is to have guests over for dinner every so often. But then all those important papers that were gathered up and put in a corner somewhere inevitably get lost.

I guess if you're a retired family of two living in a three-bedroom house, the problem isn't for you. But if you've got kids sleeping in those other two bedrooms, you've got trouble. Which is what I've got.

After years of trying to figure out where to put all the things I just couldn't throw away, I have come up with a solution. It's known as "Debby's stack." And it's famous in our house.

Debby's stack is right beside the telephone in the corner on the kitchen counter. It takes up about two feet of counter space, maybe a little less in the summer when the kids aren't bringing papers home from school every day.

Debby's stack never gets any higher than 18 inches. That's because there is a wall cabinet directly above the stack. So periodically I have to go through and toss certain items to make room for more junk.

Some things get dumped on Debby's stack as soon as they enter the house. Annual reports, alumni news letters, the most recent snapshots, junk mail.

Occasionally a bill gets in Debby's stack by mistake, and doesn't surface until the telephone company is on the line wanting to know why last month's statement is still outstanding. It's hard trying to convey Debby's stack over the phone to an angry bill collector.

There's nothing wrong with being stacked

Debby's stack isn't just limited to paper. That's where you're likely to find the Scotch tape, the bottle opener, the glue, and often the car keys.

Whenever something's missing in our house, everyone knows to check through Debby's stack first. We've found old homework assignments, dividend checks, bank statements, the instruction book to the new Cuisinart (which is now old), two or three hair brushes, the boating charts, and our pocket calculator.

The top three-inch layer on the stack is usually pretty current. But once you get any lower than that, you never know what's going to turn up.

Last week the pile was spilling over the edge of the kitchen counter and starting to swallow the phone. I decided it was time to whack it down to size again.

At four inches I found the little screen net that's used to clean out the leaves in the swimming pool. No wonder the pool has looked a little crowded lately.

At five inches I found copies of our 1980 income tax return. I wonder how many baby sitters now have a complete financial picture of our net worth?

At six inches, I discovered a bunch of food coupons that had expired in November, 1979. And my receipt for the 1980 Publisher's Clearing House give-away. And a note that one of the baby sitters had written down, telling me to "Call Barbara, it's urgent!" I wonder what Barbara wanted, and I wonder what year she called?

Eight inches from the top, I found the papers for our dog. We've had the dog for a year, and the registration papers were never returned to the American Kennel Club. Does this mean our dog is, as they say, illegitimate?

77

Somewhere near the bottom of the stack, below the thank-you card I never sent and above the 1978 Christmas cards, is a newspaper article on organization. I must have clipped the story, but I don't know when.

Just as I started to read the helpful hints on organization, my daughter walked in from school, threw a bunch of papers on the kitchen counter, and started for a snack.

That was the excuse I was looking for. I stuck all my treasures back in my stack and helped her eat some cookies. I guess deep down, I know I'm never going to get organized. So why fight it?

21
I should have seen it coming when the moving van arrived!

What do you do with a broken roller skate, one wagon wheel, the handle from a shovel, a rotted rudder and a chipped pane from a jalousie window?

That's the collection of treasures my daughter came home with last week, proud as a peacock.

"Where did you get all this junk?" I asked her, surveying the bits and pieces she had carefully displayed on the garage floor.

"The people down the street are moving, and he gave me all these neat things," she said with all the excitement of a treasure hunter.

I knew then that we were headed for trouble.

"Well, just what do you plan to do with these 'neat' things," I said, not really sure I wanted to hear the answer.

"I'm going to use the wheels from the roller skate to make a go-cart, and the handle can be used to pull it, and the wagon wheel can be a steering wheel, and the old rudder can be a brake, and I'm not sure what this piece of glass is going to be," she smiled.

I told her she'd better get her acquisitions off the floor of the garage before her dad came home, or she might not be able to find them at all.

Later that week she came home with a stack of old magazines, a few musty books and a plastic briefcase that was split open at one end.

"Just how many more days before they move out," I asked her as casually as I could.

"Oh, they're not leaving until they get rid of a lot of their stuff," she said, showing me the rusted screw driver with a "beautiful yellow handle."

That's what I was afraid of.

On Thursday she carried home a ruby red glass vase that had to have come from a carnival huckster's shelf, an ashtray with a picture of a U.S. Steel steel mill engraved on the bottom, and a deck of cards that must have been left over from World War II.

"I wonder why they aren't taking all these treasures with them," I said to my daughter.

"The man said he always liked me and he wanted me to have this stuff," she said, obviously elated.

I thought about not letting her out of the house during the weekend, but that proved impractical. So on Saturday she brought home a dusty old picture frame with a yellowing photograph of the old RCA Victor dog, with his ear to the speaker.

"Won't this look cute on my wall," she said.

It was clearly time to put a stop to this charade. I was running out of patience and my daughter was running out of storage space, but my neighbor wasn't running out of junk.

"I think you've taken about enough from that nice man," I said to her as gently as I could without laughing. "Maybe you should let him distribute these goodies to some of the other people."

"That's a good idea," she said, handing me a broken yardstick and a Teresa Brewer record.

Then she gathered up the old saw with the missing teeth, the dusty and discolored stuffed fish and the miniature plastic slot machine, dumped them into the broken baby carriage, and wheeled everything down the driveway and up the street.

"Where are you going?" I asked her.

"Im going to share some of this stuff with the neighbors," she said. "It's not fair to keep it all myself!"

I must say I was relieved to see the moving van finally arrive on our street. I don't think I could survive any more giveaways.

22
Bathroom battles make me flushed

It's hard for me to believe that our family ever survived in a one-bathroom house.

Why just the thought of it is enough to make your hair stand on end.

Back up north the single bathroom in our first little house taught me more about cunning, diplomacy and tact than I could have learned in five years with the State Department.

The problem was simple.

If my husband and I were both following different schedules it was smooth sailing. But let us both need the bathroom at the same time and watch out — all hell would break loose.

"I have to be first in the bathroom," my husband would implore. "When you go first the mirror is so steamed up I can't even see to shave."

"You've got a lot of room to talk," says I with my dander up. "It takes me two hours to set and dry my hair but all I have to do is walk in this bathroom after you've had a shower and in two seconds my hair looks like I just shook hands with Reddy Kilowatt. You'd think I'd invented the Frizzies!"

"Why don't you take your shower at night so we wouldn't have these problems every morning," he would say.

"If you think that's such a great idea, why don't you do it," I'd reply, and soon we were back to square one.

It was about then I decided to take the diplomatic approach.

Breaking a time-honored tradition, I decided to get up a little early in the morning to make his breakfast. Then just as soon as his alarm would go off and he was about to step into the bathroom, I'd yell "Good morning, honey. It's breakfast time. You'd better come down right now or your eggs will get cold!"

For a week or so it worked like a charm until he figured it out and got tired of eating alone.

Bathroom battles make me flushed

"Why don't you sit down and join me," he said one day in earnest. "Fix yourself some breakfast. I'm tired of eating alone."

Feeling a little guilty, I decided to comply. I had just sat down to breakfast when he suddenly got up from the table. "I'll be right back. I want to get the morning paper."

Thirty minutes later he returned to the table with his paper, still in his pajamas but clean shaven and his hair neat as a pin. He sat down without saying a word and proceeded to read the paper.

It cracked me up!

T'was then and there we promised each other we'd never again live in a house with one bathroom.

I can look back on those days with amusement. I can smile remembering the night I served sauerkraut and pork at a NewYear's Eve party and later watched the line form at the door of our single bathroom.

When we moved into our second house, it had one-and-a-half bathrooms and we really thought we were living in luxury. But the day we moved to Florida into our three-bathroom house, we thought we had died and gone to heaven!

While some people may consider a three-bathroom house a bit extravagant for a four-person family, I don't. Frankly, I think a ratio of one bathroom-per-child is a requisite for the continued sanity of any family.

Never again would we have to fight for a bathroom. Our two daughters could primp to their hearts' content. My husband could shower for hours on end without having to worry about my hair. And I could discover the meaning of that hitherto unknown word, "privacy!" Oh, it was a dream come true.

Now, there are some problems that crop up.

Even though each child has her own bath, they still haven't mastered the skills needed to clean a bathroom. So there are just that many more sinks coated with Crest, mirrors decorated with soap designs and gritty bathtubs covered with sand.

Bathroom battles make me flushed

My husband and I still share a bathroom so we still have the disputes over how to roll up the toothpaste tube. Furthermore, it never ceases to amaze me that out of a family of four, I am the only one who seems to know how to put on a new roll of toilet paper! And in three bathrooms, no less!

Then despite the fact that we have enough bathrooms, I seldom find myself alone in my own. If the children aren't busy asking me questions, my husband has to shave or brush his teeth. You almost need a policeman to direct the traffic in and out.

But a real all-out bathroom battle didn't erupt again until recently when our friends, Harvey and Mary and their two children, flew down from Buffalo for a visit.

When I arrived at the airport that Thursday, it was not only our friends that got off that plane, but in-flew-enza!

It seems the Sunday before Mary had intestinal flu but the next day she felt better and forgot all about it.

On the day they were to leave for Florida, the baby threw up on the way to the airport. They told themselves he was just carsick and it would surely pass. When the same thing happened on the plane, they decided he was probably airsick. But that night when he tossed his cookies at the dinner table, there was no denying it any longer — that kid had the flu!

The next day the baby was still under the weather while the rest of us felt fine. But at 2 a.m. things started popping! I awoke from a deep sleep and made a beeline for the bathroom. Suffice it to say, it was the first of countless visits. I, too, had caught the flu.

Shortly thereafter another child came down with it and around 3 a.m. I caught a glimpse of

Harvey as he sprinted like a racehorse to the guest bath!

By 8 a.m. everyone but Mary was sick.

Well folks, let me tell you. If you thought we had bathroom problems before, you wouldn't believe it now. It was so bad we had to laugh. For two solid days we tore back and forth to the bathrooms and poor "Typhoid Mary," as my husband called her, was stuck taking care of seven invalids — all of whom thought they were at death's door!

Luckily, however, this tale has a happy ending.

Like comrades in arms, we survived the "Battle of the Bathrooms" and emerged from it closer and better friends than ever before!

23
My house was designed by Frank Lloyd Wrong

My home must have been designed by the same guy who invented the sardine can.

It's fine for a retiring family of two. But if you've got a kid or two, forget it.

It's big enough to entertain eight people standing up. But if they want to sit down to eat, it's out of the question.

It's roomy enough if your hobbies are reading and bridge. But if you like to play ping-pong or shoot pool, you're in big trouble.

There's nothing wrong with my home that an additional six large rooms and a basement wouldn't cure. You'd think a four-bedroom house would be plenty big enough for a family of four. But take my word for it — it isn't!

I think my house was designed by Frank Lloyd Wrong.

All the walls are too close together. And each day they're closing in on us a little more.

My three-year old daughter is still in a crib. And it's a lucky thing. There isn't enough space in her bedroom for a bed. Just a crib and a toy chest spilling out over the top.

In my bedroom, there is just enough space for a king-size bed and a queen-size dresser, but there's no room for us to hold court.

Frank Lloyd Wrong never heard of a playroom. So my nine-year-old daughter has to entertain her friends in her bedroom. That's okay now, but in a few years I have a feeling my husband won't be so hot on the idea — especially if those friends are boys.

We might as well have the open classroom concept in our house. Everytime you turn around, you rub noses with a child. They're everywhere. You can't get away from them, even though there are only two.

The kitchen is the hub of our house, no matter how hard I try to avoid it. If I'm cooking in the kitchen, I can usually hear what's going on in the rest of the house. That's because the rest of the house is usually in the kitchen.

At a dinner party, I become the featured entertainment. Guests in three different rooms can watch me cook their meal. They have no choice.

And serving the food can be a real problem. If I serve it buffet-style, there's no place for the guests to sit. If I have a sit-down dinner, there's no place to serve the food.

Our "dining area" holds eight uncomfortably. Anything above that number and I'm in real trouble. It's pretty hard to carry on polite dinner conversation with eight in the dining room, four in the living room and two on the patio outside.

When we bought our house, the real estate agent told me it was a "dream kitchen." Everything is in easy reach. How right she was. Oven, kids, refrigerator, kids, sink, kids, cabinets, kids.

Our garage looks like the inside of a Mayflower moving van. Boxes piled on boxes, all with labels that have been altered, crossed off or mismarked. If I want to find the good brass candlesticks, my husband can tell me right where they are.

"Check the big yellow box above the washing machine, and if that's not right, check the brown

My house was designed by Frank Lloyd Wrong

box under the white box near the work bench," he says.

Work bench! I never saw a work bench. It must be under those boxes on the far side of the garage. If we ever have to put our car in the garage, we're in big trouble!

I guess the only solution is to use the same decorating scheme the people in the model homes use — single beds in every bedroom, a sofa and one chair in the living room, a table for four in the dining room, and stick a "For Sale" sign on the kids.

That's what Frank Lloyd Wrong had in mind all along.

24
Florida's state pest is driving me buggy

Believe it or not, there are a few things in Florida that can drive a new resident buggy.

For women, it may be the fact that you have to set your hair every day because of the humidity. For men it may be the need to wax the family car every month to keep the blue roof from turning to pale gray.

But nothing is more exasperating than learning to live with bugs.

I'm not talking about mosquitoes. I've learned to tolerate those little pests, with the help of 6-12, Cutter's, Raid and the mosquito patrol.

I'm talking about the bugs you share your home with.

Don't deny it. I know I'm not alone in this one.

There aren't many people who feel comfortable watching a roach crawl out from under the bread box and across the kitchen counter ... next to your mother-in-law, who is fixing a plate of hors d'oeuvres ... to feed 20 guests who are standing nearby. All eyes are on the roach. That gives you the perfect opportunity to slink away — and find the insecticide.

I don't know all the bugs in my house on a first-name basis. I don't even want to know their family history. All I know is that I don't like to see them peeking out at me from under the furniture and inside the cabinets.

My first experience with Florida's bugs occurred the day we were moving into our home. I was unpacking boxes and putting away pots and pans. I opened one kitchen drawer and a roach scurried out and across the kitchen floor.

"What's that?" I screamed.

"Oh that's just a palmetto bug," one of the movers said calmly.

He told me I shouldn't worry about a few palmetto bugs.

"Those are roaches," I yelled. "Why can't anybody admit that those are cockroaches?"

That's when I discovered that most people in Florida can't really deal with the fact that they share their homes with roaches. So they euphemistically call them palmetto bugs. Life is so much more pleasant that way.

As I started to pack my bags, my husband agreed to seek professional help. The exterminator arrived the next day, full of information and insect spray.

She's taught me lots of interesting things. For instance, did you know that certain species of cockroaches produces as many as 400,000 offspring in a one-year life span? And did you know that scientists estimate that if all young cockroaches born within a two-year life span lived, their weight would outweigh the planet earth?

With little tidbits like that, the exterminator has been a regular guest in our house ever since. She stops by every month and we swap bug stories. I'm an old hand at it after three years.

And while she hasn't eliminated the bug population entirely, she has been able to make my home less inviting for those uninvited guests.

Sure, I know there's a hotel for roaches located right under my stove. I've seen them scurry in and out, lugging their little suitcases. I've even stepped on the doorman. But what can you do?

The exterminator tells me to keep the house clean and make sure there aren't any crumbs on the floor. Have you ever tried to live in a house with two small kids and a dog, and keep the crumbs off the floor at the same time? Forget it.

It took a while, but I'm finally getting to feel more comfortable with bugs, even when I turn off the light.

In fact just last month we had some house guests from the north. During the second day of their it, I heard a shriek coming from the bathroom. I ran in to see my friend standing on the toilet, pointing to something big and black in the tub.

"There's a roach in your house!" she screamed.

"That's not a roach," I told her calmly.

"That just Hector, our pet palmetto bug. Give him some bread crusts and he'll go away. Nothing to worry about."

You see, even I'm using the old palmetto bug ploy these days. The trouble is, I'm beginning to buy it!

25
Swap the Gulf for Lake Erie—you've got to be kidding!

The older I get, the more hotels leave me cold. The beds are usually lumpy. The showers waver between a cold drizzle and hot steam. Seldom are there enough towels, and never are they big enough to dry an adult.

The ice machines never seem to work, and the Coke machines always require three quarters, and I usually have only two.

Just once I'd like to walk into a hotel room and see a pretty bedspread and clean carpet. Instead, I usually toss and turn my way to sleep imagining what the room would look like in shades of pink and green instead of orange and brown.

My biggest objection, however, is the price. For $50 to $75 a night, I expect fresh flowers, breakfast in bed, a newspaper at my door in the morning, courteous and efficient service, and some change back when I check out. Usually, all I get is the bill.

So you can imagine my excitement last year when I opened a letter and read:

"How would you like to vacation in Barbados, stay in a hilltop villa with a panoramic view of the sea, four bedrooms, maid, gardener and car at your disposal — all rent free?"

How indeed? Is the pope Catholic?

"There's no catch," the letter said. "Simply sign up for our home exchange service and stop spending money on hotel rooms. If you want to swap your home for a villa in France, a townhouse in London or an apartment in San Francisco, send us a description of your home and we will arrange an exchange."

I couldn't believe it. Home swaping was made for me. It might take a month or two to get my house clean enough to exchange, but how could I pass up an offer like this.

I quickly assessed my own home and sent them this description:

"Lovely 4-bedroom, 3-bath home in Southwest Florida. On narrow but picturesque canal. Pool needs cleaning, grass needs cut. Dog goes with the house, but little care required. Half-hour from beaches, 5 minutes from McDonald's. Exchange for anything with enough room for family with 2 small kids."

I think the home exchange company must have had a hard time finding a category for my house. It was nearly a month before they contacted me about my first exchange possibility.

It read: **OHIO, 2-bedroom townhouse in suburbs of Columbus. Close to movie theaters and Ohio State Fair grounds. Two-hour drive to Lake Erie. Pool shared by 200 other apartments. Interested?**

"What happened to Paris and London," I wrote back to the home swapping service. "I want something more exotic than Columbus, Ohio."

They advised me to be patient, that something else would come along. And it did, a month later.

BANGKOK, traditional teak house with all modern conveniences, in countryside 45 minues from central Bangkok. Air conditioning, garden, 2 bedrooms, 1 bath. Interested?

Swap the Gulf for Lake Erie—you've got to be kidding!

"I can't afford to travel all the way to Bangkok to spend a week in a teak house with air conditioning and a garden," I cabled the company. "I don't even want to go to Bangkok."

Be patient, they said again. They'd work out some sort of exchange for us.

Weeks went by, and I started cleaning my house in anticipation. Then another letter arrived, and I was glad I hadn't wasted too much time cleaning.

TIBET, ancient palace once used by Dalai Lama. Remodeled, new plumbing, 37 bedrooms, formal gardens, overlooking mountain lake. Attached stable with large herd of goats for transportation. Unique vacation opportunity. Interested?

"Just what is a family of four going to do in an ancient Tibet palace for two weeks," I wrote back. "There's more to life than riding goats for fun, you know!"

My third rejection evidently didn't sit too well with the home exchange service. They suggested that perhaps I was being too particular, and that with what I had to offer, I should be willing to accept something less than a villa in France or even an apartment in San Francisco.

Their suggestion:

OHIO, 2 bedroom rustic cabin in Dille's Bottom, with spectacular view of Ohio River at your front window, surrounded by collapsing coal mines and scenic steel mills. Outside facilities just 20 yards behind residence. Just minutes away from the thriving metropolises of Wegee, Businessburg and Crabapple. Interested?

"No thanks," I wrote back. "I grew up in that area and it took me 25 years to get away. I have no desire to vacation there, even to rekindle memories. Got anything else?"

Well, the home swapping agency that promised to arrange an exchange must have decided I was nothing but trouble. Their final letter stated they were having a difficult time finding someone interested in swapping homes with me. The letter was accompanied by their final offer.

SOUTHWEST FLORIDA, 3-bedroom, 2-bath house on picturesque golf course with pool and Jacuzzi. Half hour from the beach, 10 minutes from McDonald's. Interested?

"Thanks," I wrote back, "but no thanks. The Jacuzzi sounds interesting, but I'd rather be closer to McDonald's. I guess I'll just stay home."

26
You think you've got problems!

The older I get, the wiser I become.

It's taken me more than 35 years, but I've finally learned that to solve a problem, you first have to determine who the problem belongs to.

I learned this marvelous technique in a little course I took last year on dealing with children and keeping your sanity. But I find it works well with the whole world.

Let me explain by way of example.

You're in a long line at the bank teller's window with your four-year-old daughter, waiting to cash a check. She's a little upset because there are no toys to play with, so she starts screaming something like "I want to go home!" and begins kicking the man in front of her.

Is it your problem or your daughter's?

Well, it looks like your problem, but actually it's your daughter who has the problem. She has to deal with being bored in a more acceptable manner.

Now, when the man in front of your daughter turns around and mutters something like "why can't people learn to control their kids," who has the problem?

Again, it looks like your problem, but in reality the problem belongs to the grouch in front of you. If he doesn't like to be kicked in the shins by a little girl, then he should move to another line.

When the bank president finally comes over and asks you to leave the bank because your daughter is bothering the customers, who has the problem?

Well, the problem finally belongs to you, especially if you don't have enough money to get out of the parking lot. You've got to learn to deal with humiliation.

Now that I have this great knowledge, I realize that everyone in the world likes to pawn their problems off on other people. I should know. I've been shouldering a lot of unnecessary problems for a lot of years. Mothers are good at that, you know.

But once you realize that the problem doesn't really belong to you, you can sail through life with new innocence.

At last I can take the family out to dinner in a nice restaurant and not worry about the kids' misbehaving. If spilled milk bothers the waiter, that's something he has to learn to cope with. If the woman at the table next to ours is offended at having my daughter watch her every bite for a good half-hour, that's her problem, not mine.

I suppose you're thinking to yourself, "that's her problem, not mine!" See how nice life can be when you lay it off on someone else?

Another interesting thing I've discovered is that whoever mentions the problem first effectively hands the ownership of the problem to someone else.

For example, if you and your husband are sitting by the pool and your husband says "I wonder if there is enough chlorine in the pool," he is handing you the problem of finding out if there is enough chlorine in the pool.

In other words, it was his problem that he forgot to test the pool last weekend, but he decided to make it your problem so you would have to do the work.

If you want to hand the problem back to him, you can say something like "I haven't seen the pool testing kit for a month." That means it is now his problem to find the pool testing kit and you don't have to worry about it.

Of course, he can always counter with something like "I'd like to find the pool testing kit, but my foot's asleep and I can't move it." The problem is now back on your side of the court.

The two of you can bat it back and forth all day while you watch the pool water turn brown from

You think you've got problems!

lack of chlorine. Or one of you can finally accept the problem, and the work that it entails.

Unfortunately, now that I have discovered the joy of determining who owns the problem, my children are now using the same technique. And it's a little unnerving.

Last week I was yelling at my daughter to get her room cleaned up, pointing out that she couldn't even make her way into the closet to get any clothes because the toys were stacked so high.

"But mother," she signed. "I like everything just where it is. It's your problem if you can't deal with my messy room. It's not my problem."

Kids can be ridiculous!

As nice as "problem ownership" is, there is a danger that if you use it too much, you may end up married to a martyr.

Let's say your husband is hanging wallpaper. You walk by and casually observe that the third strip from the corner is upside down.

Your husband groans because he knows he made a mistake but won't admit it. So he tries to hand the problem back to you.

"Can't you live with one strip of flowers growing down into the floor instead of up into the ceiling," he asks, raising his eyeballs inside his head.

He knows the answer before he even finishes the question. So he walks over to the wall, dramatically rips off the strip of wallpaper, and gives you the evil eye.

You have effectively established that the problem is his, but he has now become a martyr, accepting the problem and trying to make you feel guilty for wanting all the flowers to grow the same way — up.

If you refuse to feel guilty, you have no problem. But once your husband sees the faintest sign of

99

remorse, he has given you the problem for ever and ever.

But that's not going to happen to me. I may be naive, but I'm no fool!

27
In hock, and stranded at the dock

Boats are a lot like children. They demand constant attention. They cost more to take care of than you ever dreamed you could spend. And they never perform when you want them to.

When we decided to go "nautical" two years ago, we thought it wise to get a new boat and motor rather than take over the problems of someone else.

You see, my husband is about as mechanically minded as one of the Three Stooges. If it requires more than a key to start the motor, we're out of luck.

Boat salesmen have a knack for spotting families like ours. They know just the right things to say.

"Don't worry, you won't have any trouble with this motor. It's guaranteed for a year. Nothing to take care of, no parts to change. Just put gas in it and off you go."

So of course we bought the boat. How can you pass up something that's easier to take care of than a lawnmower?

I'll have to admit, that first year was trouble-free. Kind of like every new product you buy ... no problems until the warranty is up.

Then one day we had friends over for a trip to the beach. We spent 15 minutes packing the boat ... towels, food, drinks, ladder. Everyone piled into the boat, my husband turned the key, and nothing happened.

"Maybe it's your battery."

"Have you checked the spark plugs?"

"Is the fuel line blocked?"

"Maybe it's the water pump."

"Are you out of gas?"

If the battery wasn't dead to start with, it was after my husband spent five minutes trying futilely to start the engine. We spread everything out on the back yard and had a picnic, watching as the repairman spent the afternoon working on our boat. He had the last laugh, however. His bill was $115, and no amount of wine could get him to alter that figure.

Things went along fine for several months after that tune-up. But the next time the engine wouldn't start, my husband thought the repair bill was too steep. He decided to try it himself.

It took him five minutes and 15 pages of the owner's manual to figure out how to remove the engine cover.

"Why do they write these instruction books for engineers?" he yelled, trying to figure out the difference between a distributor and a starter.

I guess the maze of wires and screws was just too much. He put the engine cover back on, swallowed his pride, and called the friendly repairman.

Over the past year, things have gotten worse. Usually the boat starts with no trouble when it's just our family that's going for a ride. But once you invite anybody else, the boat seems to know the difference and refuses to start.

We've developed a regular routine lately, more out of necessity than anything else. If the engine doesn't start when you turn the key, my husband usually swears something under his breath. Then he takes the engine cover off and stares hard at

In hock, and stranded at the dock

the inner workings, trying to decide just which cable is at fault.

He jiggles some wires, takes the spark plugs out and cleans them, and then tries to start the motor again. If it still doesn't start, he looks over at me with that "why did we ever buy this boat" look, says something like "I've tried everything I know how to do," and slams the keys on the floor of the boat.

Often, that will do it. When the engine hears those keys hitting the floor of the boat, it knows it has won another battle. If I stick the keys back in the ignition and turn them, the motor often starts right up.

Of course this puts a lot of strain on a marriage. I figure the boat is pitting me against my husband. Whoever files for divorce first gets custody of the boat!

If this routine fails — and it sometimes does — I usually say something like "Have you checked the battery cables?" I know by this time that the only thing that keeps my husband from kicking the engine is the $3,500 price tag, so it's important to maintain a light, breezy tone in any remarks I might make. Any guest worth his salt knows to keep quiet during tense moments like this.

If, after scraping a month's worth of corrosion off the battery terminals, the boat still doesn't start, it's definitely time to regroup and plan an alternative activity.

I've noticed that our family isn't the only one suffering through the "boat problem." My father has had so many problems with his boat that my mother finally bought him a little plaque to put on the wall of the boat. It says "A boat is nothing but a hole in the water, surrounded by wood, into which you throw money."

They say the best two days in your life are the day you buy a boat and the day you sell it. There's probably a lot of truth to that.

But what worries me is that second day. I have this deep-seated fear that when it comes time for someone to buy my boat, the thing won't start. And then I'll never get to experience that final ecstasy.

28
Fishing in troubled waters

Fishing with two kids in your boat is about as much fun as folding eight loads of laundry. No, make that 12 loads.

We only take the kids along on these fishing

trips every two or three months, but each time I forget just how bad an experience it can be.

Take last weekend, for example.

We loaded up the boat, packed a picnic lunch, got a couple dozen shrimp for bait, and set off.

I knew from the minute we left dock that it was a mistake.

"Mommy, my hat fell in the water!" my three-year-old daughter screamed as we made a wide U-turn in the canal to retrieve a soggy, pink object that once resembled a hat.

Once we got out in the river, the problem seemed to be just which "fishing spot" we would select. There were four suggestions and they were about as far apart as you can get and still remain in the same county.

Once we got to our location — the "captain's" decision, I might add — it was time to get out the fishing rods and start the action.

"Mine is the green fishing rod," my nine-year-old daughter said.

"No, MINE is the green one," the three-year-old yelled.

"You don't have one," my husband firmly told her, "but you can help me with my fishing rod."

She didn't seem impressed.

"I'm a big girl now, and I can fish myself," she said proudly, and then she pouted in the far side of the boat, which wasn't far enough away.

After we decided just which fishing rod belongs to which person, the more subtle problems began.

"You fish from the front of the boat, and we'll fish from the back," I told my daughters.

"I want to fish on the same side as you," one shouted back.

"Be quiet," my husband said as forcefully but quietly as possible.

"Why? There's nobody around," my daughter said.

"There'll be no fish around either if you don't stop shouting," my husband shouted.

"Will you put a shrimp on my hook?" my daughter asked.

"You've got to learn how to do this yourself," my husband said.

"I can't stand to reach into the bait bucket," she said. "Yuck!"

"Here's a shrimp," he said, handing her a nice big live bait.

"EEEEEeeeeee!!!!!!! It's so squirmy," she screamed.

"Be quiet!" he screamed.

"Here, I'll bait your hook," I told her, grabbing the rod before my husband could wrap it around my daughter's neck.

By this time the three-year-old had her hands in the bait bucket and was flipping shrimp into the river with glee.

"STOP!!!" my husband yelled. "That's all the bait we've got!"

"Daddy, will you get my line unstuck. It got caught in that tree over there," my older daughter said.

"How did it get in the tree?" he asked.

"The wind must have been blowing," she said with a smirk.

"I'm thirsty," the three-year-old said in that whining tone that you know can only be stopped by a drink of water.

"I've caught a catfish," my other daughter squealed.

"Oh, no," my husband said. He's the only one in the family who can get catfish off the hook, and that seems to be all we ever catch.

"When are we going to eat?" the three-year-old asked.
"Will you put another shrimp on the line?" the other one asked.
It went on and on.
"I have to go to the potty."
"I'm hot!"
"Oh, no! Another catfish!"
"These bugs are itching me!"
"When do we eat?"
"I couldn't help it. The pole fell in the water."
"Is that our bait bucket floating over there?"
"Who spilled all these hooks?"
Finally my husband said "The next time we go fishing we're going to leave the kids with a sitter!" And with that, he turned the key and we headed for home, as quickly as possible.

We arrived home with just one fish. I don't have any idea what kind it was, but we all felt an obligation to eat it.

As my husband was cleaning the fish on the dock, my daughter looked down at the insides of the fish spilled out on the cement.

"Oh, boy," she said. "I'm going to take that to school for show and tell."

And that's no fish story.

29
Cupid takes a holiday after the honeymoon

Valentine's Day is for lovers.

No, make that "Valentine's Day is for young lovers."

In fact, if experience has taught me anything, that should read "Valentine's Day is for young, unmarried lovers."

I hate to make any rash generalizations, but once you've got that gold band on your ring finger, Cupid seems to take a holiday every February 14th.

I'm sure there are still some married women over 30 who will be getting Valentine presents this year. Like Ann-Margaret, for instance. But on the whole, the flowers will be delivered to those pretty young things with frizzy locks and frisky walks — the swinging singles.

I'm not too old to remember the good old days when the florist truck would stop at my house with a bouquet of flowers on Valentine's Day. Of course in those days I was just wearing an engagement ring, not a wedding ring.

The first year, my husband-to-be presented me with a dozen red roses. I remember thinking what a wonderful life it was going to be, with vases filled with long-stemed roses in every room of our vine-covered cottage. I also remember my mother listening to my visions and laughing. Now — 14 years later — I know why she was laughing.

Cupid takes a holiday after the honeymoon

The first year we were married, my husband brought home one rose on Valentine's Day. "It represents one beautiful year together," he said.

It's the thought that counts, I muttered to myself as I got out the bud vase and put away the larger silver urn I had polished to hold the dozen roses I never got.

He got all the way up to five roses on our fifth year, but I think he began to realize then that the price of long-stemmed roses was going up at a faster pace than the years of our marriage. By the time of our 25th anniversary, he would be paying $100 for two dozen roses.

So on our sixth Valentine's Day together, he came home with a dozen Sweetheart roses. You know the kind. They're smaller (and cheaper).

"My, how cute," was all I could get out. "Let me see if I can find a little vase."

The next year he brought home some "everlasting" roses — the red silk kind that will last as long as our marriage. Maybe even longer!

Then the following year it was an African violet plant, and I knew we were hitting the skids. I have nothing against African violets, but who needs them on Valentine's Day?

For a few years after that I got a box of candy and a card. Last year it was just a card. As usual, I overreacted. I took the tie I had bought him and cut it in half, right through the big red heart.

This year I happened to see an article in one of those family-type magazines that stressed the importance of good communications in a marriage. I decided that was the right approach. So I tactfully left my husband a list of Valentine gift suggestions that would make my heart go pitter-pat:

- A cleaning lady for one day. She could scrub the grape jelly off the kitchen floor, scrape the bubble gum off the screen door, clean out the oven and wipe off the windows as I sat watching the soap operas all day.

- A weekend without the kids. We could eat by candlelight and soft music instead of the chattering of little voices. We could have breakfast in bed and not worry about one kid getting butter all over the sheets, another kid putting her foot in the

scrambled eggs, and the dog knocking over the glass of orange juice.
- A day totally to myself. No clothes to wash, no children to feed, no trips to the store, no arguments to referee. I could relax and read whatever I wanted — and I don't mean Mother Goose.
- A dozen pairs of new underpants. Let's face it. This is one little luxury that we never allow ourselves.
- A dozen long-stemmed red roses. I defy you to find a woman who doesn't deep down in her heart want roses, no matter what the cost!

30
Requiem for a guinea pig

Into each life a little pet must fall.
Our pet happened to be a little guinea pig, which had an eventful, if somewhat short, life.

Squeaky came to our house as a surprise birthday gift for my older daughter. And it was indeed a surprise.

We hadn't had a pet in our family for several years, so Squeaky was pampered with kindness for the first few days. There would be battles about who would hold Squeaky, who would feed Squeaky, who would play with Squeaky, and of course, who would clean Squeaky's cage.

I would never have guessed it, but the guinea pig fit right in. I guess that says a lot about our family, doesn't it?

Actually, Squeaky was an ideal pet. You didn't have to house-train it because the little critter stayed in the cage all the time. And it would eat just about anything.

Our guinea pig got the name Squeaky because when anyone petted the animal, it would squeak. I never knew if the squeak was one of appreciation or terror. Knowing my kids the way I do, however, I'd lay odds on terror!

My daughter had the job of cleaning Squeaky's cage. She would put Squeaky in the laundry tub so it couldn't get away. Squeaky was a fast little devil! Then she would scrub the cage in the front yard.

One day I put a load of wash in the washing machine, not noticing that Squeaky was in the laundry tub. Well, the wash water started draining out of the washing machine right into the laundry tub and down the drain.

It was lucky I noticed Squeaky, stroking for dear life in the laundry tub. I took the animal out, dried it off with a hair drier, and comforted it for about an hour.

The Clorox lightened Squeaky's hair a bit, and the fabric softener made the hair so soft that it was like having a new pet.

I got to like Squeaky so much that I decided it might be fun to have some more around the house. A litter of little guinea pigs would be an educational experience for my kids, I told myself. And they were pretty excited about it.

So I took Squeaky to the pet store to find out how you go about adding to the family. One store owner checked Squeaky and said it was a girl, but he didn't have any male guinea pigs he could loan out for the necessary few weeks.

Another pet store owner, however, came up with a young male guinea pig that would be the apple of any eye. He added, however, that the male might still be a little young to breed.

Well, we took the male home, put it in the cage with Squeaky, introduced them, and waited. The two little creatures didn't hit it off right away. There was a lot of fur flying at the start, but they soon settled their differences, and we began to have hopes for a family.

Weeks went by and nobody noticed any apparent difference in their behavior, or in Squeaky's tummy. But you never can tell, so we waited to see what developed.

About a month later we decided the whole project was a failure. Either the male was too young, or there was just no love in their courtship.

I took the two back to the pet store, explaining that I wasn't sure, but I thought that sweet little Squeaky was still a virgin.

The pet store owner decided to conduct a little examination of his own. He pressed a few points on Squeaky's tummy and then burst out laughing.

It turned out that all our hopes for Squeaky getting pregnant were in vain. Squeaky was a boy!

So we had wasted two months trying to mate Squeaky with a male guinea pig, but we did learn to call her "him."

I was the one who discovered that Squeaky had gone on to his great reward. And I worried about how to tell the kids.

My sister was visiting us at the time, and she had already had experience at informing her kids about the death of their cherished parakeet. So she concocted an elaborate explanation leading up to the news that Squeaky had died. That way the kids would hear the explanation and not be so shocked by Squeaky's demise.

"Now kids," she began. "You know how everyone has a soul. Well, when people and animals die, their souls go to Heaven but their bodies remain behind. And that's what's happened to Squiggles," she told my daughters.

At the mention of the name "Squiggles," my husband and I looked at each other and broke into laughter.

I guess the laughter eased the pain for my daughter, somewhat. She took the news rather well.

And as we stood beside Squeaky's little grave in the garden next to the air conditioner, my daughter's only words were, "Why didn't you tell me he died before I cleaned the cage today?"

31
Puppy love

I may be a slave to tradition, but I believe every child should have a dog, no matter what the neighbors say!

So turning a deaf ear to the screaming neighbors with the fancy gardens, we bought a dog. That was one year ago, shortly before the guinea pig died and just after we had the carpet in the whole house cleaned.

Our dog is a shih-tzu, and she lives up to it in every sense of the word, if you catch my meaning! You'd think that after a year the dog would be house-trained, but either she's too smart or I'm too stupid.

The dog doesn't seem to make the association between the door and the bathroom. When duty calls, she doesn't hesitate. I guess that's why we decided to call her Muffin . . . she leaves little muffins all around the house in unsuspecting places. It makes vacuuming a real challenge, believe me.

In case you've never heard of a shih-tzu, you're not alone. They're pretty hard to find.

I had to call all over the eastern United States before I found one that I could afford. You see, Muffin has a tooth problem. It's called an overbite.

Muffin's mother took one look at those little teeth sticking out and said, "knock $100 off the price tag and send her South."

Middle Age & Other Spreads

When Muffin arrived (via an Eastern Airlines jet from Pennsylvania) my friends thought I was crazy.

"You just got one kid out of diapers," my friend Jeanne said. "Why do you want to submit yourself to that torture again?"

She was right. I was crazy. But I didn't realize it until it was too late. I'd forgotten just how messy a puppy is.

Muffin is a tiny dog. Even after a year's growth, she is still too short to jump up on the sofa. That's one of the good things about her.

On the other hand, in the first six months Muffin was staying with us, her dental bills more than made up for the $100 savings on her original cost.

Getting a puppy isn't like getting a baby. You have nine months of planning before the baby arrives. If you had nine months to plan for a puppy, you might decide to change your mind somewhere during the third week.

We decided the best place for Muffin to sleep during her puppyhood was in the bathtub. That way she couldn't get out and deposit her little presents around the house during the night.

Of course that decision, although basically sound, put one bathroom out of commission for at least four months. You know, of course, what happens if you wake up a little puppy in the middle of the night. You spend the rest of the night keeping it company.

Gradually everyone got tired of waiting to use the same bathroom, so we kicked Muffin out of the tub and into the kitchen at night.

Fleas were also something I didn't plan on. But in Florida fleas take to dogs like roaches take to the kitchen. On the third trip to the vet for dipping, I met a nice lady with a small dog similar to Muffin.

"Honey," she told me, "I've got just one piece of advice for you. Don't let your dog outside."

Don't let your dog outside, I thought. That's outrageous! Dogs have to go outside.

"You keep your dog inside and train her to go on the paper and you won't have any fleas to worry about," she told me.

Well, as ridiculous as it sounded, anything was worth a try. And sure enough, my dog hasn't been outside since. Of course the kids have to be real careful where they step on their way to the swimming pool, and guests tend to open their eyes a little wider when they see our patio area.

Just recently I decided it would be fun to have some more little puppies around the house. I'm a glutton for punishment.

With Squeaky's experience fresh in my mind, I took Muffin to the vet and asked his advice.

"This dog shouldn't have puppies," the vet said. "There's no sense carrying these teeth on for future generations. And even if you did, you would have trouble selling the puppies. Why, this dog's teeth are so bad the people should have given you the animal free."

Well, I didn't know whether to be humiliated or defensive.

I took Muffin home, we sat down on the floor together, I opened up a package of Swiss cheese, and we stuffed our faces in sorrow.

I decided that despite the buck teeth and the bad breath, despite the fact that the carpet in the living room is awash with vinegar, despite the slobbering and licking and jumping and scratching, Muffin is worth every penny of her price.

She looks like a little stuffed toy, but no stuffed animal could survive all the love and affection

Muffin gets from my two daughters. Their devotion to that silly little dog makes it all worthwhile.

32
Ho, ho, ho?
No, no, no!

Who could ever put a price tag on Christmas? My husband, that's who!

He could listen to "The Twelve Days of Christmas" and give you an itemized accounting of the total bill for maids-a-milking, gold rings, calling birds and French hens before the needle lifts off the record.

I don't like to use the word "Scrooge," but there is a certain resemblance. It starts way before Christmas when he sees the price of toys.

"I refuse to spend $29 for a wooden truck," he says. "All it is is a block of wood with some wheels on it. What happened to the creative toys we used to have when I was young?"

"Why should we spend $36.50 for a doll that wets itself? We've already got a child that wets herself. This doll would set a horrible example. Let's spend the money on diapers instead. Better yet, let's put a price tag on the child."

"Fifty dollars for a computer that teaches kids how to spell! I could get a tutor to do that job for $30. Better yet, let's save the money and have spelling bees every night after dinner."

"You mean the electric train that my father bought for $25 when I was a kid now costs $275? And it's not even made of metal? Maybe we should look for a little red wagon instead."

The trauma of the toy prices goes on for months before Christmas arrives. But the Christmastime cost consciousness really becomes an issue when it's time to pick out a tree.

Call me old-fashioned, but I refuse to give in to the lure of an artificial Christmas tree. I may resort to plastic money to buy my live tree, but I will never be happy with a plastic tree.

It took the first five years of our marriage to establish the fact that no shiny aluminum tree would grace our living room, no matter how cost-efficient it may be. That means we fight the battle over a live tree every year.

I've always been a stickler for searching out every lot to find the best tree available. Cost is no object when I'm looking for the tree that will fill my home with Christmas spirit.

"It should be full, tall, and perfectly shaped," I tell each tree vendor.

"And not too expensive," my husband is quick to add.

Middle Age & Other Spreads

Ho, ho, ho? No, no, no!

He shops for Christmas trees the way I shop for canned peaches — the biggest for the cheapest price. It's a long day, believe me. And usually not very pleasant!

"I like the $12 Douglas fir," he usually says after being stuck by so many Christmas trees that his arms look like they have the measles.

The $12 Douglas fir is shaped like a bowling pin and has a enormous gap in one side. But it is 5 p.m. and the sun will be going down soon, and he wants to get the whole ordeal over with.

I, on the other hand, think the best buy is the $28 Scotch pine that we saw at the Methodist church parking lot. It was two feet taller than our living room ceiling, but we could always chop off some of the bottom.

We race back to the Methodist church parking lot, only to find out some woman in a VW paid cash for the tree and carted it away.

"That settles it," I say. "We'll get the gorgeous eight-foot pine at the mall. Let's hurry and get there before it's gone."

Four lots and two hours later, we plop down $30 for a tree that is nearly perfect, pay another $2 to have it delivered because it is too big to fit in the car, and head for home.

Now my idea of decorating the house for the holidays is to fill every corner of every room with color. The aroma of fresh pine should fill the house. Bright red candles and Christmas lights should reflect the spirit of the holidays. After all, when there's no snow outside to get you in the mood, you have to go a little overboard inside, right?

My husband's idea of decorating the house is to put a spotlight on the wreath hanging on the front door. A low-powered spotlight, at that.

"Let's buy a few more strings of outdoor lights

and put them on the hedge along the front of the house this year," I said last Christmas.

I thought he was going to have a stroke on the spot.

"Are you kidding?" he said. "Those lights are selling for $6.50 a string this year. And do you know how much extra electricity they would eat up? That surcharge from the electric company really adds up. Let's be patriotic this year and forget the outdoor lights."

Last yeat I noticed that as various bulbs burned out, he would neglect to replace them. And while I like to turn on the outside Christmas lights at dusk and leave them on until midnight, I usually caught him quietly sneaking over to the switch at around 8:30 p.m. each day to turn them off.

Last Dec. 1, I noticed my husband was working on his annual Christmas list.

"That's $30 for the Christmas tree, and two new strings of lights at $6.50 each makes $43, plus $20 for the cards and $9 for the stamps makes $72, and . . ."

"Listen," I said. "This is only the first week in December. You better not start that list now or you'll never make it to Christmas. With inflation as bad as it's been this year, you're liable to go into shock by Dec. 20th."

His only retort was to remind me that I could have saved $7 by buying this year's Christmas cards last January when they were having the after-Christmas sales.

"Come on," I said. "No one likes to receive a musty smelling card with mildew-remover stains all over the inside."

I guess there's no way to avoid it. When Santa Claus says "ho, ho, ho," my husband starts counting up the dough, dough, dough.

33
'Tis the week after Christmas . . .

**'Tis the week after Christmas, the house is a pit.
Toys fill every room, kids are throwing a fit.**

Nothing is worse than the post-Christmas blues. After weeks of expectation, everything comes to a quick halt and we are all forced to deal with reality.

The kids go back to being the monsters they really are. After all, Santa Claus won't be checking them out for another 11 months. Why should they be good?

All those toys they wanted so desperately before Dec. 25 are just heaped in the closet, or on the living room floor. Despite four new games, 12 new toys, five new books, an electric train and a new bike, there's still "nothing to do!"

The needles have dropped from the tree once so green.

They've clogged up the vacuum and now it won't clean.

The $30 Christmas tree now looks like it cost about $4.98. Someone forgot to put water in the tree holder. Now just whose job was that, anyway?

Everytime the front door opens, the beautiful wreath with the gorgeous red bow slams into the wall of the house. Pine needles cover the front hall, and the wreath looks like it got caught in the closing doors of an elevator.

**Red candle wax is splattered on the top of the table.
As for cleaning it off, no one seems to be able.**

Middle Age & Other Spreads

It's funny how long it takes you to clean the house, and how quickly it gets dirty.

The red wine that was spilled on the floor adds a little color to the green carpet.

The white ring from the wet glass of milk Santa left on the coffee table should disappear by next Christmas, with luck.

And I'm sure we won't have any trouble mending the cigarette burn in the pillow of my new chair. Accidents will happen at parties, you know!

We polished off the cookies in less than a week.

The success of our diet once again seems quite bleak.

I can't believe how much everyone eats during the holidays. I know I baked more than 12 dozen cookies for Christmas, but by New Year's Eve there wasn't one to be found. Where had they all gone? No one would admit knowing, but take one look in the mirror and you'll see a clue.

And the egg nog does wonders for the figure, not to mention the six-course Christmas dinner, the pumpkin pie with real whipped cream, and the five-pound box of candy that seems to have disappeared.

Dozens of batteries are strewn on the floor.

That favorite new toy has stopped working once more.

If I had a few thousand spare dollars, I'd invest in a company that makes batteries. Or a company that sells plastic to toy makers.

These new computer toys are the best thing that ever happened to Eveready batteries. In fact I think we bought more batteries than toys this year.

My youngest daughter doesn't even know what a windup toy is. When one of her toys stops working, she knows the battery is to blame.

The poinsettia that last week was brilliant and red
Now looks like it's wilting and soon may be dead.

'Tis the week after Christmas . . .

I don't know why I keep buying poinsettias every year. They start dropping their leaves about the same time the Christmas tree starts to droop.

I always plan to plant them outdoors in the garden, but each year I never get around to it until it's too late.

The sweater we bought Grandma was a beautiful fit. The only problem was she had one just like it.

After years of mistaken sizes and wrong colors, I've finally learned to save receipts for Christmas presents.

Another thing I learned to save is boxes. They're hard to get these days, so after the shirts and pajamas are dumped out, I put all the empty boxes in the guest room closet, right next to the boxes of bows and slightly used wrapping paper. It leaves hardly any room for guests.

Despite the high postage, late cards still arrived, And some of the messages seem quite contrived.

The stack of Christmas cards gets smaller each year. That's either an indication that inflation is hitting the card industry, or that our family should switch deodorants.

Despite the prices, there evidently are still families left who can afford to send out those chic cards made of heavy white cardboard, with an embossed dove and fourteen-carat gold lettering. Sometimes they come with silk tapestry depicting a Biblical scene. Those are the cards I put aside, but never do anything with despite my good intentions.

And then there are the snapshot cards, with a blurry photo of a family standing in front of their 35-foot Chris Craft or their brand new Mercedes, smiling with that pride of achievement. Or a snapshot of the family standing at the Great Wall of China, indicating not only wealth, but also culture.

**The bills are arriving for all of those gifts.
My husband and I are having quite a few tiffs.**
Every year it's the same question. "Do you realize how much we spent on Christmas this year?"

Now I ask you, how can you follow a budget at Christmas? It's the season you have to make allowances for. The thing the children will remember the rest of their lives.

**For two hectic weeks the house was a roar.
Now vacation is over, and it's quiet once more.**

Another copy?

Wouldn't you love to have a copy of this book to send to your relatives up North, or your mother-in-law across the state, or your friends across the street?

Well, through the magic of the U.S. Postal Service, and a little luck, **"Middle Age & Other Spreads"** can put a little sunshine in their lives, too. All it takes is your check or money order for $4.50 per copy, or three books for $12, plus 80 cents postage and handling for each book ordered. (Florida residents, add 4 percent sales tax. That's 18 cents per book.)

If you want me to send the book directly to your friends or relatives, please print their name, address and zip code legibly on a piece of paper and send it along with your order. Jot down your phone number, too, in case I have a question.

Send your order to: Debby Wood, Box 1737 Cape Coral, Fla. 33910.

Order blank for Debby Wood's "Middle age & other spreads"

Please send _____ **copies** .... $ _____
(each copy is $4.50; three copies for $12)

Fla. residents add 4% sales tax .... $ _____
(18 cents for each book ordered)

Please add postage and handling costs .... $ _____
(80 cents for each book ordered)   **Total** .... $ _____

Send to: (please print)

Name _____

Address _____

City/State/Zip _____

Phone number (in case I can't read your printing) _____

Send this order blank with check or money order to:
Debby Wood, Box 1737 Cape Coral, Fla. 33910
Make checks payable to Debby Wood

If you want books sent to other people, print their names and addresses on another sheet of paper, along with your check. We will sent the books directly to them. If they live outside of Florida, there is no state sales tax.